KIDS COLOR THEORY

Spramani Elaun

Nature of Art For Kids® Publishing
P.O. Box 443
Solana Beach, California 92075

http://www.ecokidsart.com
email: treepassion@gmail.com

This book may be purchased for educational sales promotional use.

FIRST EDITION

Designed by Spramani Elaun

Subject: Children's Art/Art Education

Library of Congress Cataloging-in-Publication Data is available upon request.

ISBN
978-0-9916264-3-4

All artwork and photographs were taken in art classroom or special art events hosted by Spramani Elaun. © 2014 All reserved.

Contributing Photographers:

Mandy Sicard
Mike Hedge
Shirley Hadley
Spramani Elaun
Shanais Pelka

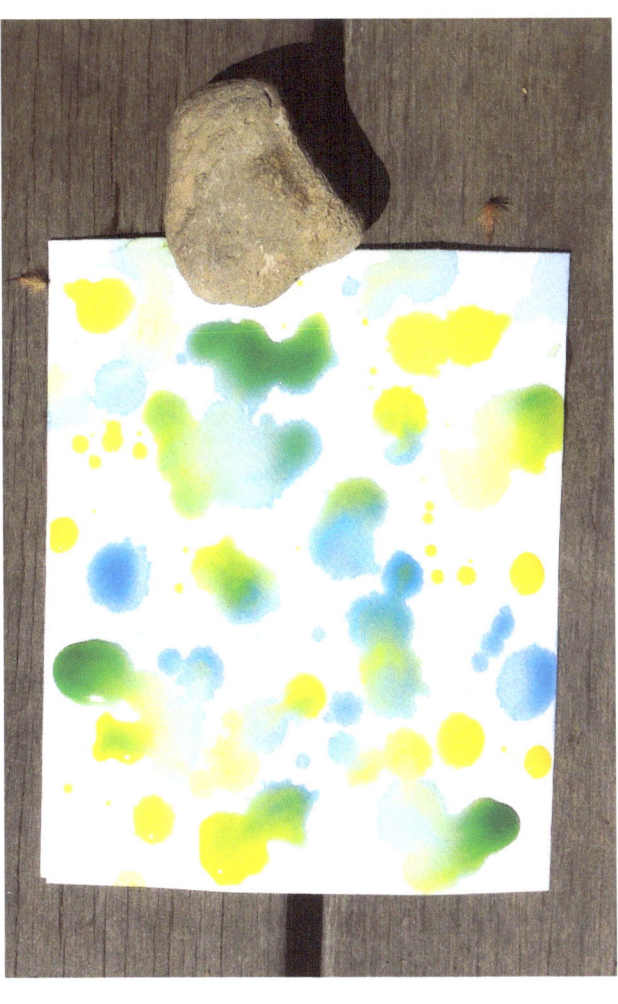

Table of Contents

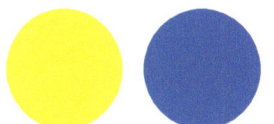

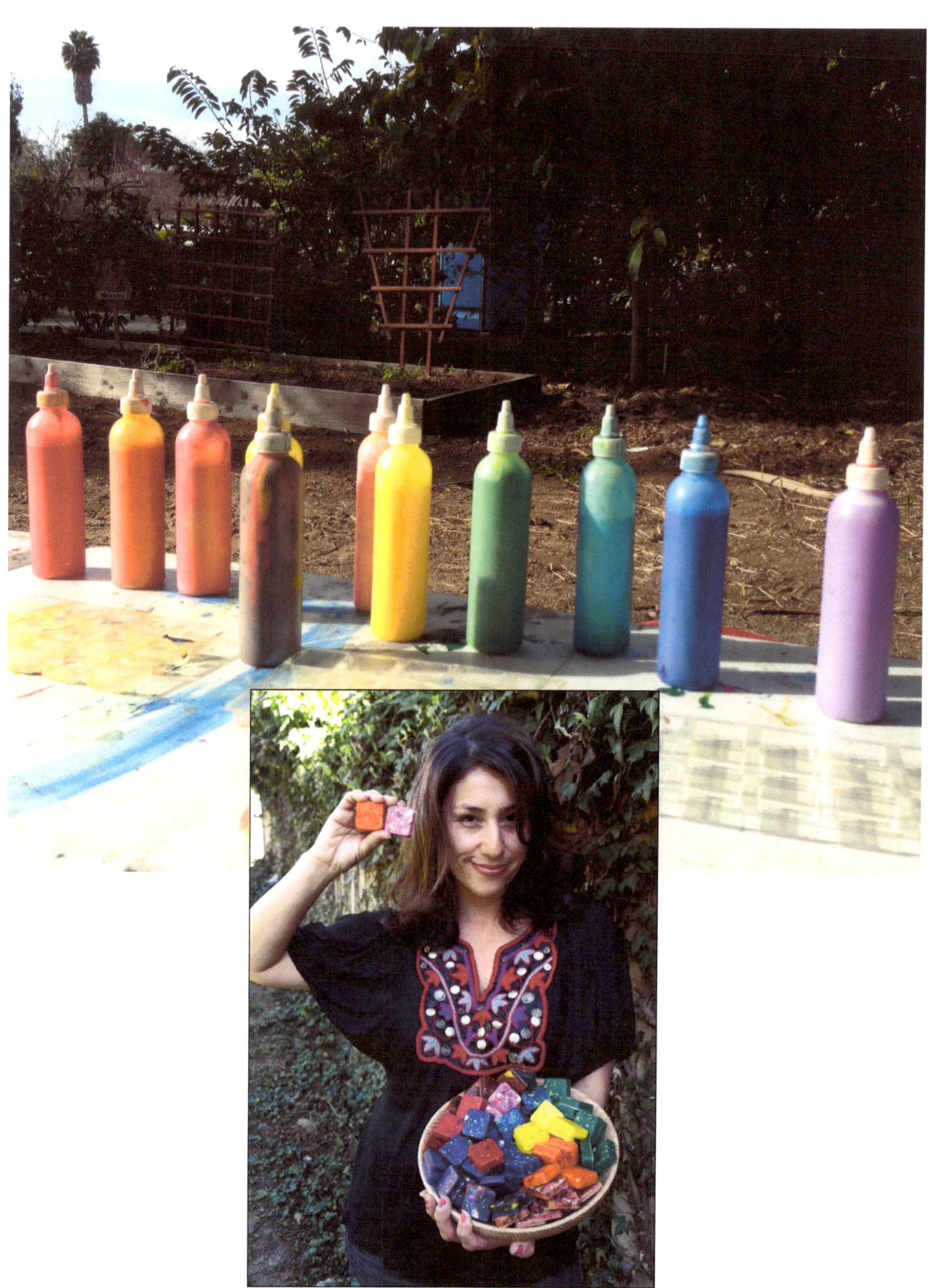

Chapter 1.

Instructors Introduction

Color has been an alluring, habitual constant in my life of designing and teaching. Working with children has been such a delight and an amazing journey, and I've spent thousands of hours exploring color alongside children of all ages. My path toward teaching young children began in the early 2000s. My focused, naturalistic observations became a natural art method for teaching children, and that is why I share my discoveries in my visual arts book series. Kids Color Theory will show and support you in how kids learn color theory in the context of art making.

Kids Color Theory Methodology

This method is not far from methods learned in contemporary artist color mixing classes. It is my natural alternative to instructing color painting in the child's younger years. It aligns with the child's growth, allowing the child to achieve skills in a safe environment without focusing on the end form, yet always influencing the child to develop artistic skills while exploring the process of color mixing.

The method works along with a chid's naturally developing sensory system and growth rate. It is not limited to the primary color wheel system alone, but embraces color technology, such as ready-made paints and color swatch systems. Kids Color Theory collaborates with early scientific rhetoric, European and American modern color theorist ideas from manual to digital color mixing, and finally, with my kids natural color theory method. If you would like to learn more about my natural art method, I recommend reading my first book, Nurturing Children in the Visual Arts Naturally.

Kids Color Theory Benefits

Mixing color is soothing and relaxing and can relieve stress. A calming effect takes place because cognitive processing is occurring while a child explores color. It's recommended that children in early childhood have a good variety of stimulating tactile activities during their sensitive periods. Working with color is excellent fine motor practice, temporal spatial learning, and a multi sensory stimulating activity. Color mixing causes high visual-auditory connectivity in the brain. This is considered active learning. Color mixing is powerful and therapeutic.

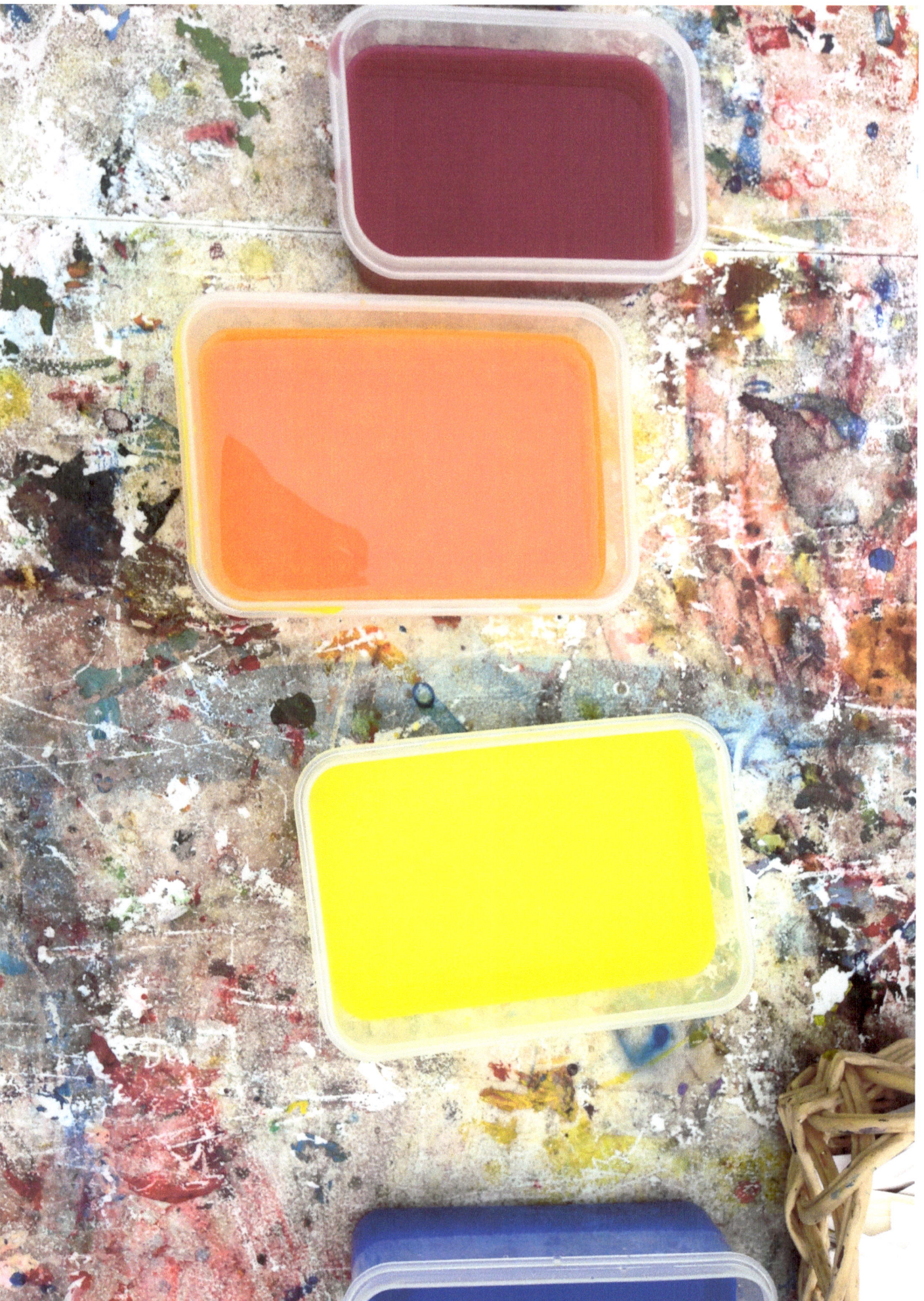

Chapter 2.

Color

Color is very important to life. From the early days of mankind we have relied on color to survive, season to season. Color helps us identify edible foods and signs of danger, and has different meanings from culture to culture. These are just some of the benefits of color. It's suggested that colors can cause different sensations and effects on our emotions. Color is what we might call magical, and only humans have the ability to experience color in countless ways in our daily life. Studying color is important for an artist, both psychologically and physiologically. In advanced color theory, artists learn to control moods in artwork by color choices and mixing skills.

What Is Color Theory?

Learning to mix primary colors into an array of color combinations is the study of color theory. Color theory skills come from observing and mixing pigmented colorants together, which allows the artist to create desired color choices or color moods.

What Is Kids Color Theory?

A simple, natural way kids learn to mix primary colors into secondary colors; mix a 12-step full spectrum color wheel, tints, shades, and tones; identify warm, cool colors, and complementary colors; color match; and work with ready-made swatches. Kids' color mixing skills come from observing and mixing pigmented colorants together, like scientific exploring.

Why Teach Kids Color Theory?

Teach Kids Color Theory mainly because children should understand nature's colors and how to recreate them in their visual art projects. This can explain how color is recreated and how it occurs in all physical things. Learning mixing skills is needed for future painting, drawing, computer generated art, and screen monitor technology. When kids learn to mix nature's spectrum of colors, it lays the foundation needed for future fine art painting lessons. Mixing primary into secondary teaches the basics to understanding advanced color theory.

Practicing mixing colors often will make painting projects more enjoyable. Teaching kids how to mix colors helps when color options are limited, and kids can mix up a variety of secondary color combinations, tints, shades, tones, and even tertiary colors, if needed. A child cannot understand color law properties unless they see the transformation with their own eyes through experiments. Lets' review how color vision is created first, before I share my Kids Color Theory core concepts.

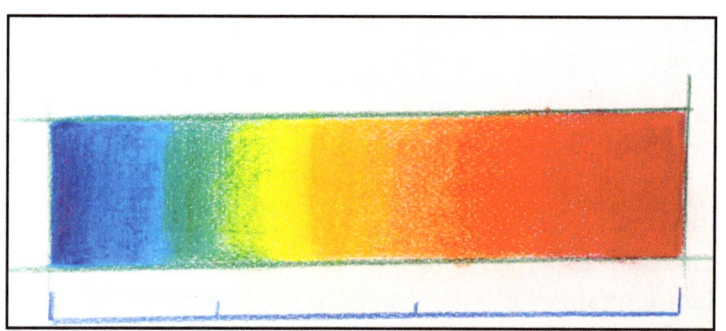

Wavelenghs 390 – 700

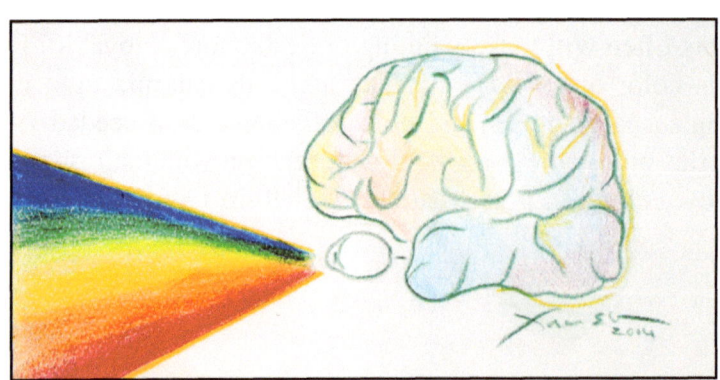

Chapter 3.

The Human Eye and Brain Together Make Colors

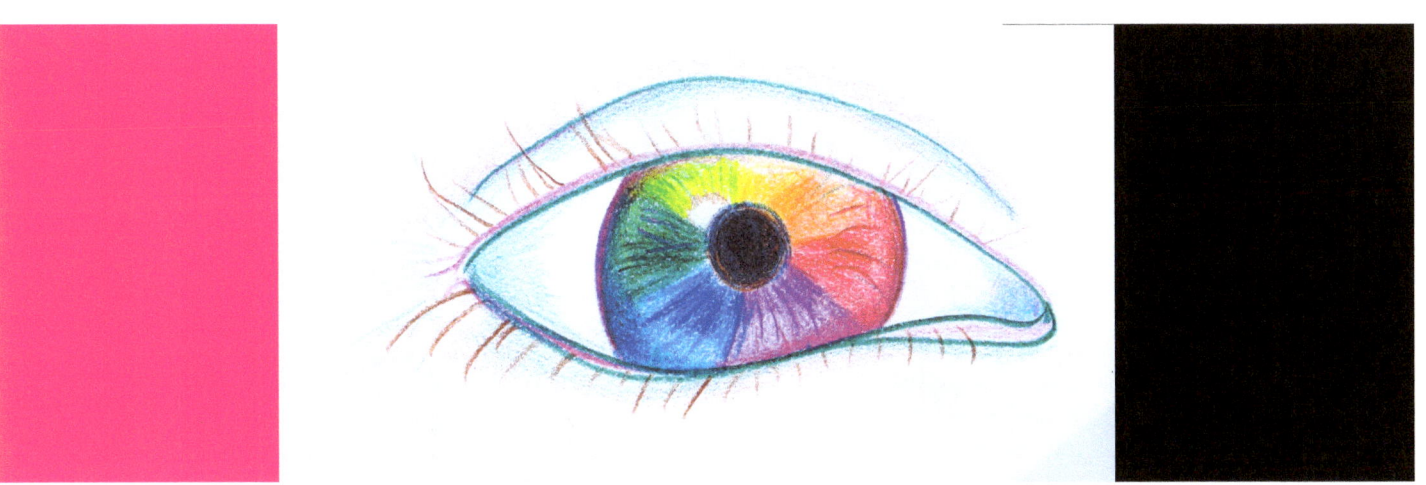

To experience color you need light. Color is present when light appears. When light travels through our retinas, this makes our human color vision possible. Our eyes sense electromagnetic wavelengths in the visible range. Different wavelength energy causes us to see different spectrums of color.

Humans can only detect wavelengths from 390 to 700. According to some scientific estimates, the human eye can distinguish 10 million hues (colors) in nature, combined in both additive and subtractive systems. Consider all the intensities of greens you've encountered through your lifetime. Human color vision is called trichromatic color vision. Our retina cone and rod receptors absorb light (electromagnetic wavelengths of radiation) through our red, green, and blue-violet cones that create the visible solar spectrum we humans experience called color vision.

The terms hue and color are interchangeable and used in the same way to identify a specific visible wavelength. Identifying different hues (colors) is how we distinguish different wavelengths, like red, yellow, orange, blue, green, and violet. Hues are also seen in a variety of intensities described as values, tints, tones, and shades.

Gamut of Hues

A color system can have a large gamut created by mixing percentages of hues with other hues.

The range of hues (colors) that can be reproduced within a color system is called gamut. Gamut also means all color combinations possible within a specific color system. Kids Color Theory is about how to teach young kids how to create their own gamut of hues from primaries and other colors.

Chapter 4.

Modern Color Systems in Place

Reproducing human color perceptions in all physical things is now possible by using color systems. Many color systems over time have been created to mimic or recreate our natural visual spectrum colors. Although these systems do exist, they could never hold a candle to the pure hues or ranges we are capable of seeing. Modern color systems today have done a great job capturing close to our natural visible colors that can be seen on earth. All man-made objects have been recreated using a specific color system. Color systems now help create color in materials, objects, photography, print, and colored lighting in screen-based technology. The color systems we use today are RYB, CMYK, and RGB, in Additive or Subtractive light.

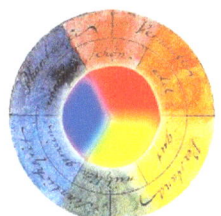

What does RYB mean?

RYB means Red, Yellow, and Blue, which are three primary hues. RYB is primarily used by mixing colorants, pigments, or dyes into color combinations, traditionally by the hand of an artist. The three primary colors of RYB can create a 12-step spectrum color wheel into a large gamut of choices. RYB is considered subtractive color, because when mixtures of RYB are overlapped, light wavelengths are subtracted (subtractive color).

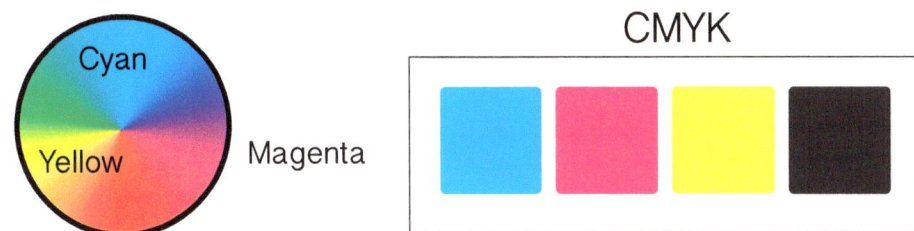

What does CMYK mean?

CMYK means Cyan, Magenta, Yellow, and Black, which are the four colors primarily used to recreate color hues in photographs, print, and screen printing. CMYK can be manually or digitally overlapped to create a gamut of hues. CMYK is referred to as four color printing. When mixtures of CMYK are overlapped, light wavelengths are subtracted (subtractive color).

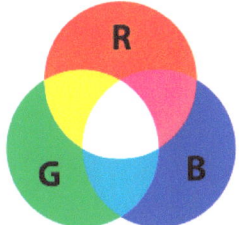

What does RGB mean?

RGB means Red, Green, and Blue-Violet, the three colors used to create screen-based technology color in televisions, computers, tablets, and cell phones. RYB is only light colors, not pigmented colorants. Beams of light are combined to create a large gamut of hues. When you are viewing color on a website, these colors are created by the RGB color system. RGB is considered additive color not subtractive color. When all three RGB beams of colors are overlapped, this projects solid white light. The overlapping of RGB colors is adding light (additive color).

Chapter 5.

Color Theories

Many color theories have been formulated as far back as 492 – 432 BC, all the way through the first half of the 21st century using different color systems. Color theories have gone through many transformations, from different theorists through the centuries, and from influential scientists, psychologists, and artists, such as Newton, Goethe, Ostwald, Munsell, Itten, Albers, and others. Color has even been attached to ideas of spiritual and psychological therapy

Theories from Antiquity to Modern Times

Over time the artist color palette and wheel have gone through major transformation up to the chemical evolution of today. New colorants have given us the ability to expand our palette choices. The colorants we have today are far different from what artists painted with in the past.

Color theory study is drastically different from what it was in the sixteenth century. In fact, color theory today can technically be classified as state-of-the-art technology. The classical painter painted by candle-light and today's child paints by electrical lighting. The painter in antiquity worked with mineral pigments hand crafted and available only in their near region. Today, we can get commercially made colorants anywhere in the world if desired, even ready-made in the largest hue choices!

Modern colorants mostly exist because of chemistry and physics. The RYB system was actually established much later in our timeline, not in the antiquity era. The idea of studying cool, warm, and complementary color is newer.

In fact, blue was considered a warm color in antiquity (Michel Pastoureau, Black: The History of a Color, 2008). Artists in the Renaissance period did not study color theory the way artists do today.

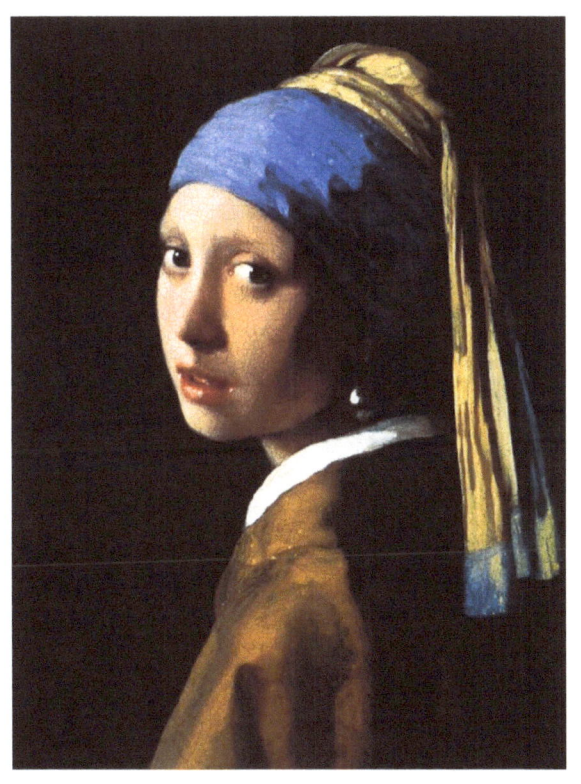

Johannes Vermeer – Duch Artisit
Girll with a Pear Earing Painting
Year 1665
17th-century
Oil on canvas – organic pigment

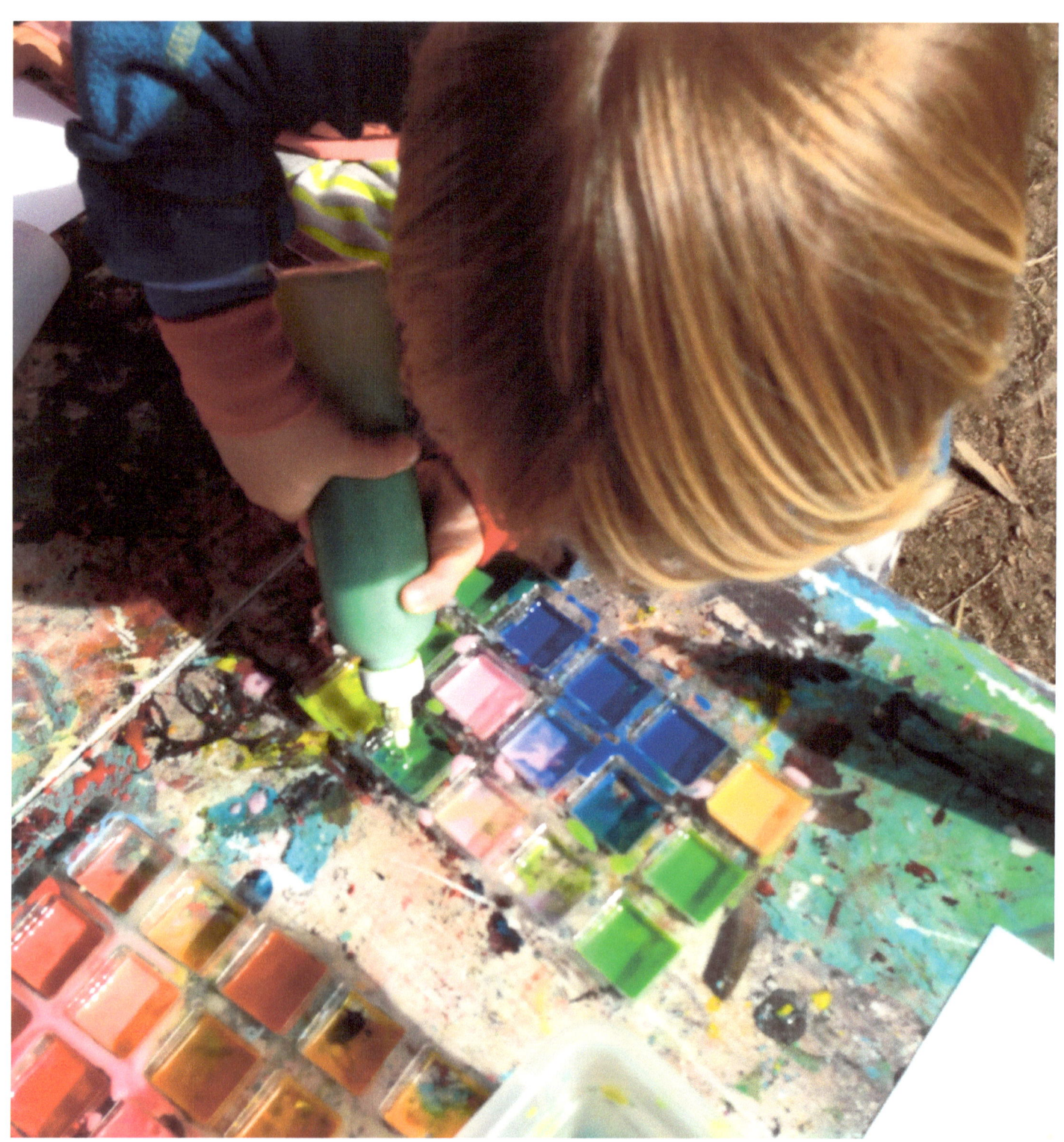

Chapter 6.

Kids Color Theory Specific for Kids

Modern color systems are beyond the young artists imagination and are hard to understand. To help young children understand how to create with color, this Kids Color Theory is a simple way to discover how color behaves and can transform into new colors. I take away the difficulty by hands-on process color mixing and matching, through each art growth phase. This is learning with relevant, simple ideas kids can relate to.

Kids learn to work with and vary colors by process mixing in real time experiences, learning the basics of color mixing by their own formulas. Understandable mixing and exploring experiences are digested in small parts. By taking away the difficulty, students can progress into more advanced mixing skills in the upper ages or grades. These easy to understand experiences nurture visual perception and spatial intelligence. This method aligns with the growth of a young child's cognitive (brain growth, visual perception), eye, and fine motor development.

Real time color mixing helps children see and understand how color choices come together with elements of design and composition. There is so much a child can explore while working through multiple sequences of color mixing exercises. Children that work with color on a regular basis become sophisticated with color over time. This dynamic spatial experience cannot be replaced by lectures, pictures, or color charts.

Artists who work on mixing color develop a deep knowledge that gives them a perspective different from that of the average person having to achieve color matching. Working through basic color mixing is a big piece of the puzzle to advance as an artist. Artists who don't know the basic concepts of color theory mixing struggle in advanced painting and digital design concepts.

Natural Child-led Discovery Process Learning

It's hard for me to separate color science and artist color theory; from the core they are both connected to our visual senses. Children can't study artist color theory without the natural analysis of physics invading their minds. Just like how color mixing works, seeing color through light or no light, how physical objects are colored, how light energy affects nature and their own spectral sensitivities to light, and how color is all linked to these ideas. I get frustrated when I think about color theory mixing lessons taught alone and not connected to natural science. Our most important discoveries of color mixing did not come from artists alone; they mostly came from scientific exploration.

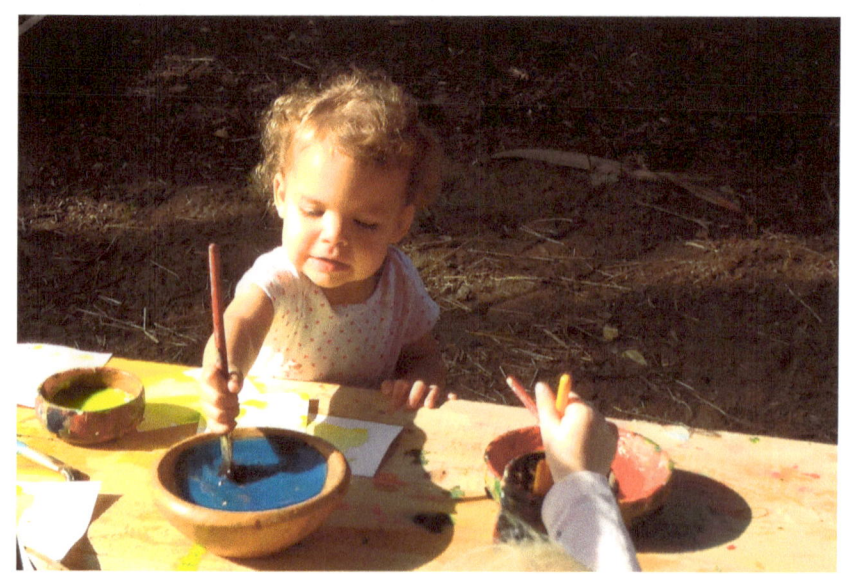

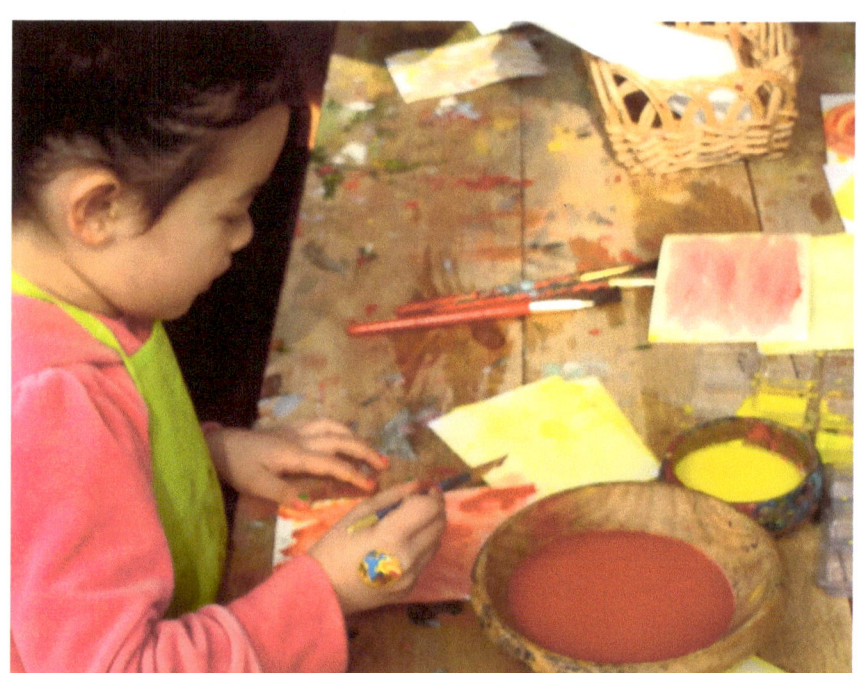

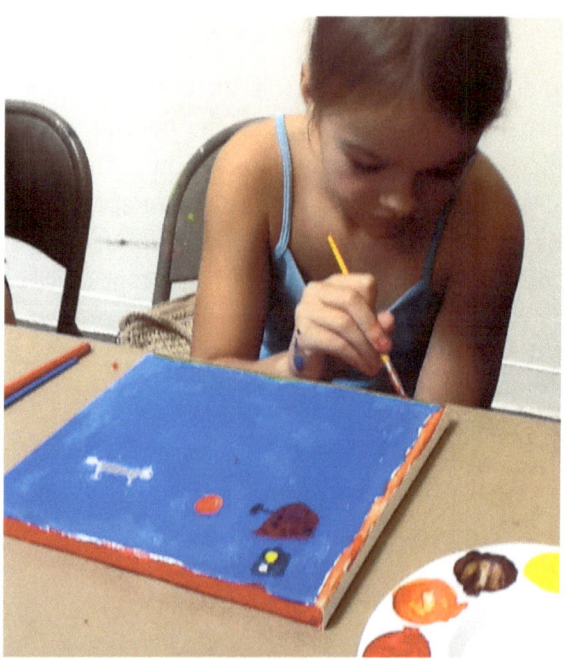

Before the meaning of color theory can be deeply understood, many experiences need to take place, starting with the basic building blocks of color information. I embrace teaching young kids color theory by allowing hours of exploration to unfold, not being disciplined in how it presents ascetically finished artworks. Young kids don't possess the knowledge we adults have; they lack color perception experiences. As a teacher or parent, we must step backwards and allow natural color play to unfold. To mix two hues together and witness a new hue is very exciting and sometimes a surprise. Kids get to see colors transform with their own eyes. A child's ability to explore with their own eyes causes good, solid understanding. Years of mixing do perpetuate advanced skills over time and naturally.

Using this discovery process learning method, kids move through progressive lessons matched with their three component skill part levels, moving through all three phases of art development. (see these definitions at the back of book).

It starts in the beginning years with no direction given, just the chance for color play. Kids Color Theory is truly presented using discovery exploration, with no explanations or remarks to notice achievements in specific hues. No expectation is required; it's more like scientific exploring and natural curious observations recording in the memory.

As kids achieve more fine-motor ability, I then direct simple mixing projects by labeling what they are trying to achieve in secondary colors and their values with analysis and observation. Then children are ready to advance skills using planned child-led color mixing projects.

When kids get more color mixing knowledge, I introduce the 12-step color wheel concepts, how to create their own shades, tints, and tones; identify warm and cool; match complementary colors; introduce nature color swatches; and select ready-made paints for their projects. Lots of child-led mixing prompts are introduced.

And finally, in the upper grades or ages, kids naturally progress to combining their discovered color knowledge with elements of design and composition. Mastery in creating color wheel charts and swatches will occur. When these building blocks of color mixing skills are laid in place, adolescents are primed for advance color theory in design, painting, digital design, or animation arts.

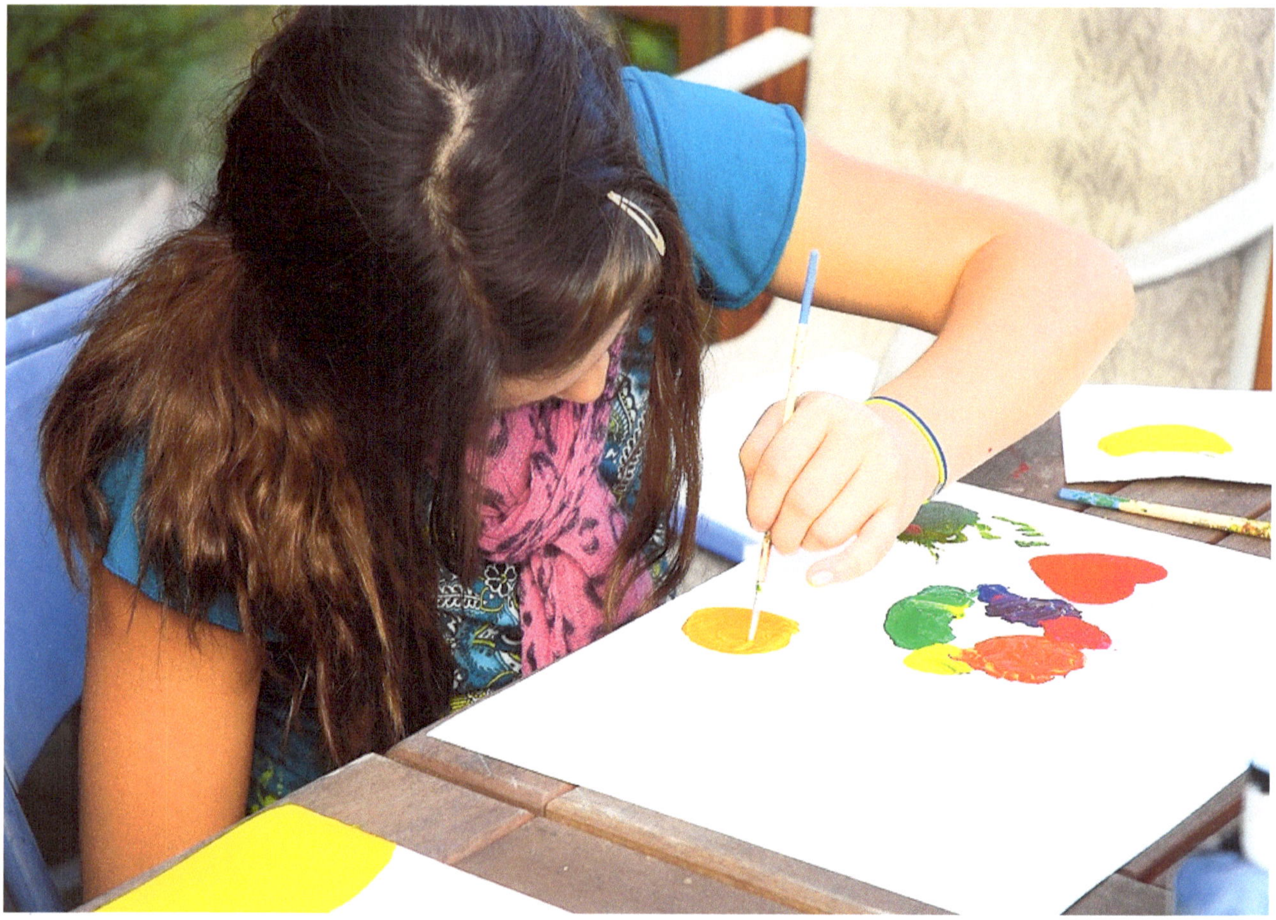

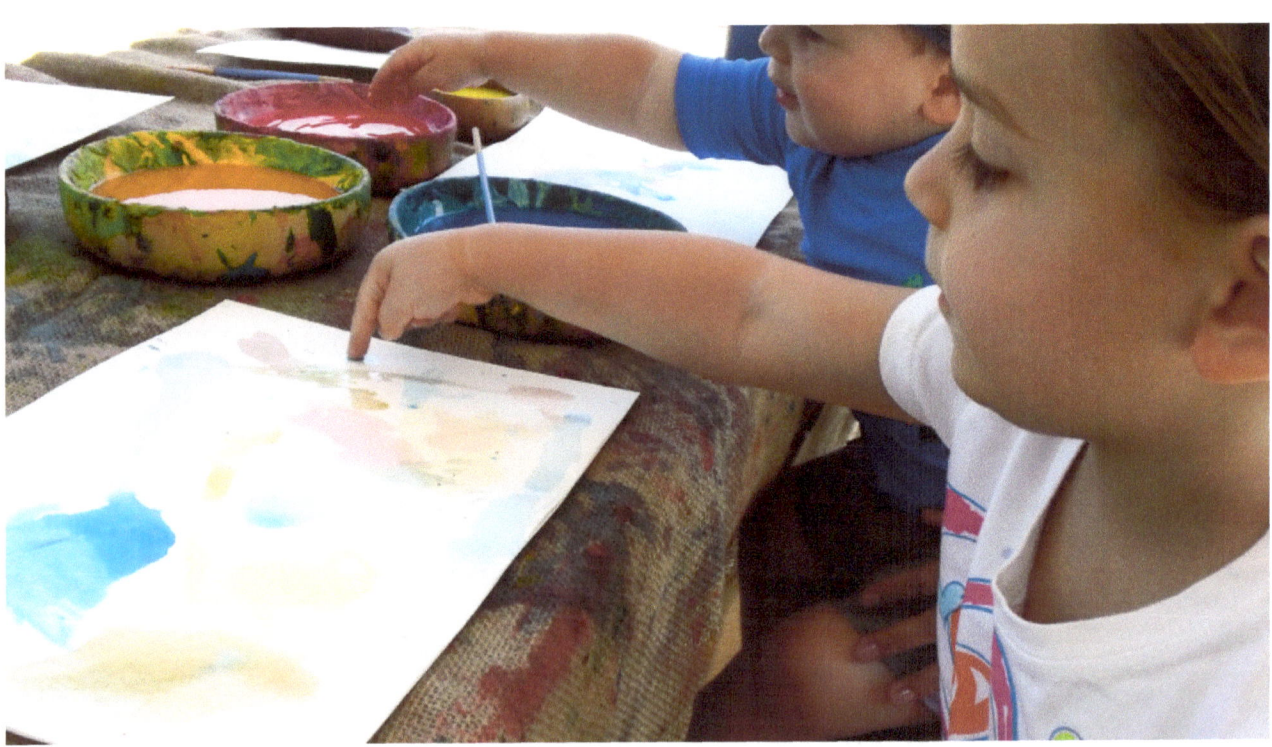

Chapter 7.

Primary Colors

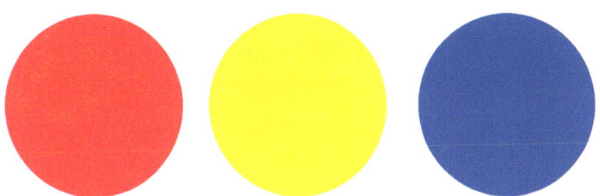

Start with RYB Primary Colors, Red, Yellow, and Blue

To ease kids into the world of color, start out in the most basic way, since children are first commonly introduced to the rainbow of colors like blue, yellow, red, orange, green, and purple. Start with the basic three primary colors. It's important kids experience color in the simplest way. Introduce primary colors red, yellow, and blue one at a time.

Afterwards, follow up with lots of opportunities to create different values in both transparent and opaque projects. Then progress into mixing primaries to secondary colors. At first, there's no control or explanation, just seeing colors achieve secondary combinations. I also introduce painting projects with primaries and secondaries ready-made, with no mixing required; this gives the child experience working with secondary values and identifying them.

It has been commonly misunderstood that primary colors cannot be created by man. But this is not true. Many pigments of reds and different degrees of yellows and blues can actually be created by other chemical colorants, and through CMYK inks. Resist telling young children primary colors cannot be created in any way. With modern color chemical technology, it is possible to make basic primaries into pigments and ready-made paints.

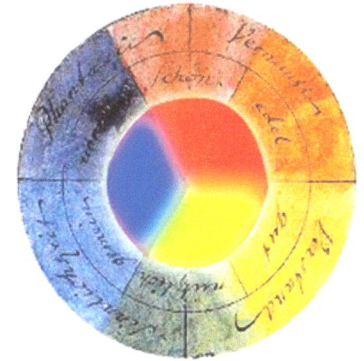

Using Color Wheel Charts

Printed Color Wheel Chart Reference Guides

Generally, color wheel charts are soft guides printed using a different color system, which is usually not the same colorants your child will be using. Following a printed color wheel chart will not be an exact match. A child is only capable of producing what is available to him or her through paints or pigments. Surfaces and hues are always changing and the gamut range will vary by different primary paint values. Having guided color wheel charts and prompts does shed some light on color mixture concepts, however.

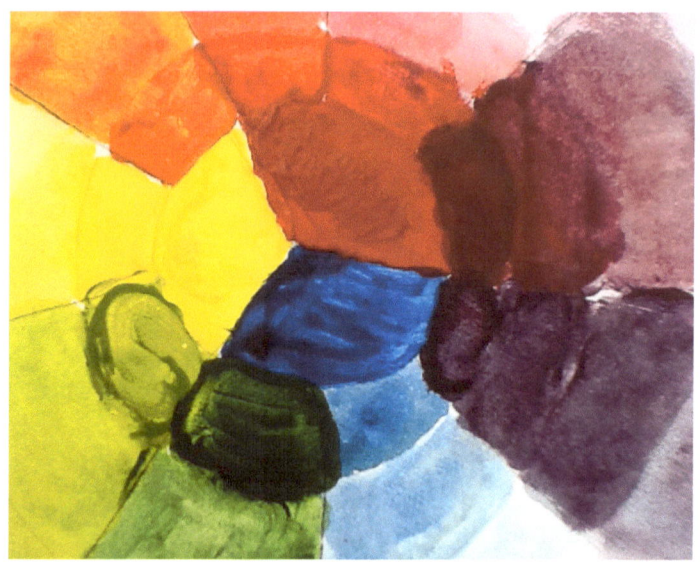 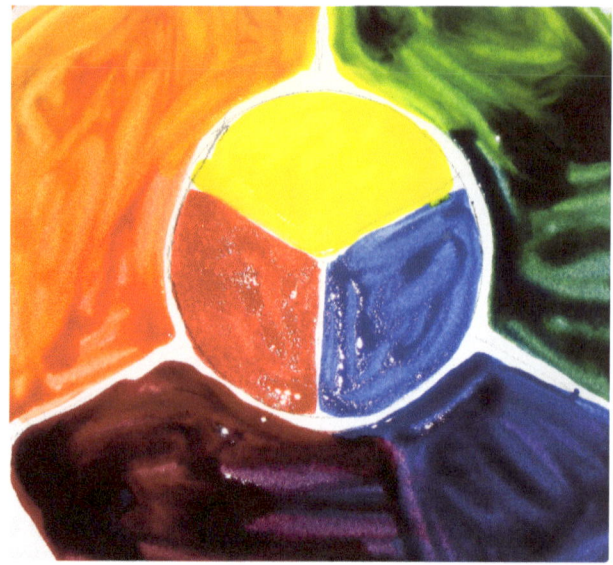

Tip:

Painted Color Wheel Chart Reference Guides

If you have paints you use regularly, I recommend creating a 12-step color wheel with those paints and present that color wheel chart as a reference. All of the color wheel charts in this book are created with my own choice of primary paints, which I use regularly in my art classes.

Buying the Right Primary Colors

When selecting primary paints, try to match your colors to the sample swatches here on these two pages. Getting primary paints as close to this sample will give kids the best secondary results. Do your best to get

close to these values; however, don't worry if you can't. You will learn that different intensity values of primaries will still promote decent secondaries. It is not critical to get exact matches. Remember, this is color exploring.

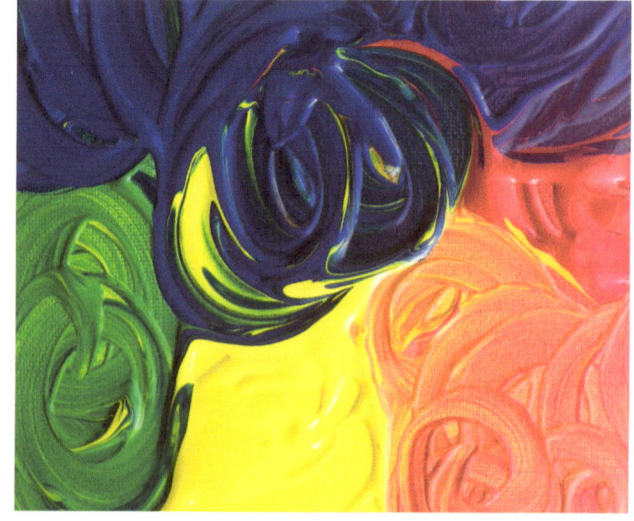

There are established color names in fine art adult grade paints that will yield excellent 12-step color wheel matching; however, I prefer that you don't use these at all. Using adult professional paints is very misleading regarding toxic ingredients safe for young children. Many adult grade paints have toxins young children should not use or must handle with caution. Do your best to seek out only child-grade paints by eyeballing and selecting primaries close to this color swatch.

RYB Primary Mixing Color Swatch

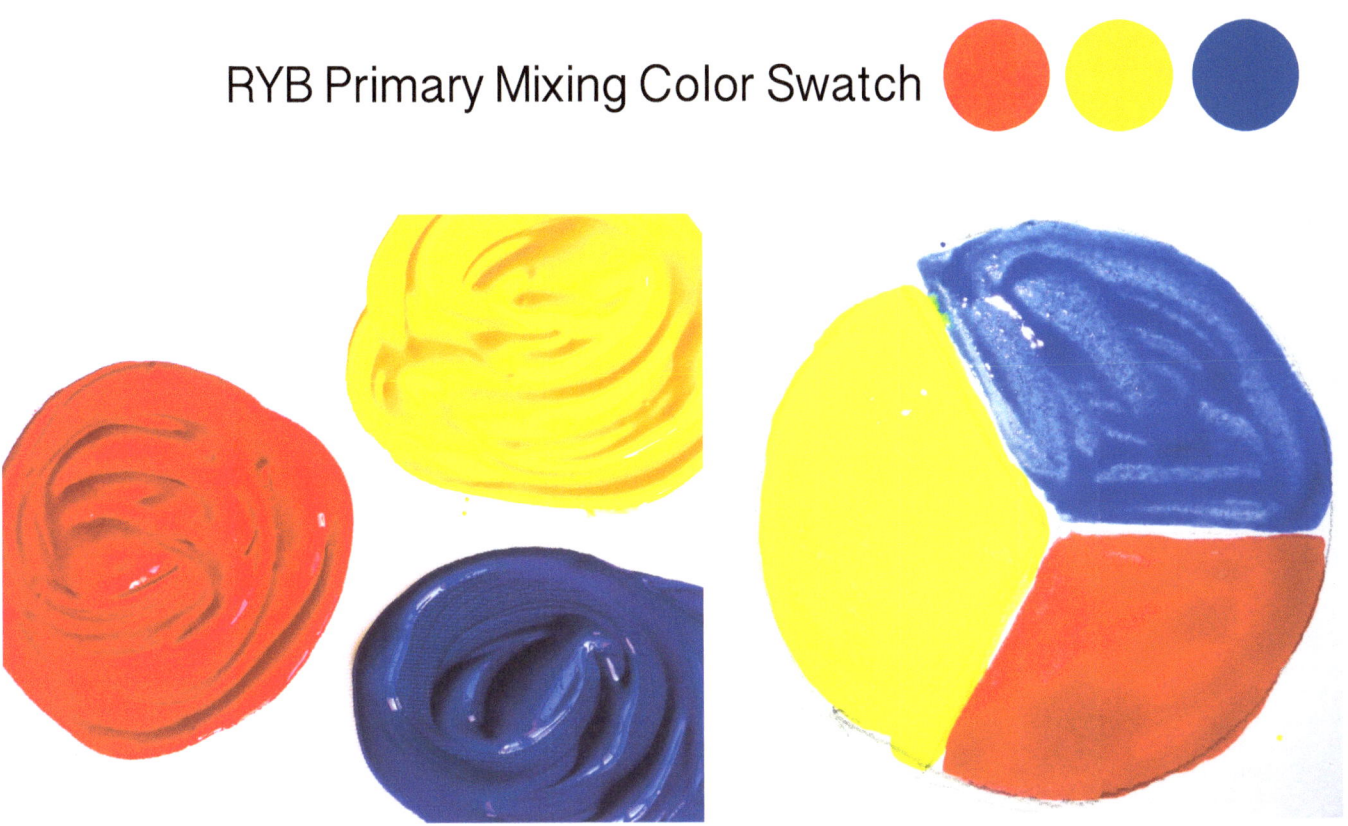

Hands-on Process Primary Mixing, True Learning

Color analysis comes from building blocks of sight knowledge. Color mixing should be filtered through the child's own mind to gain knowledge about how color behaves or works. Hands-on mixing paves the way for deep understanding of how subtractive color can be communicated on paper or canvas.

Having children make their own color wheel reference charts is the best way for them to learn color theory. Also, teaching kids to distinguish the differences between hue gradated shades comes quicker if they have a hand in making those gradual shades. The child's eye becomes sharp in identifying the levels of colors.

I don't recommend studying color theory based on past color theorist's ideas; or by lectures alone; viewing color wheel charts alone; or looking only at shaded gradations, color chips, swatches, memorization of shades; or by using color pigments that can't naturally blend into a secondary. Kids should mix colors with their own brush and witness color transformation with their own eyes. If you are presenting color theory study with only these, you are not providing a proper color theory study kids can benefit from.

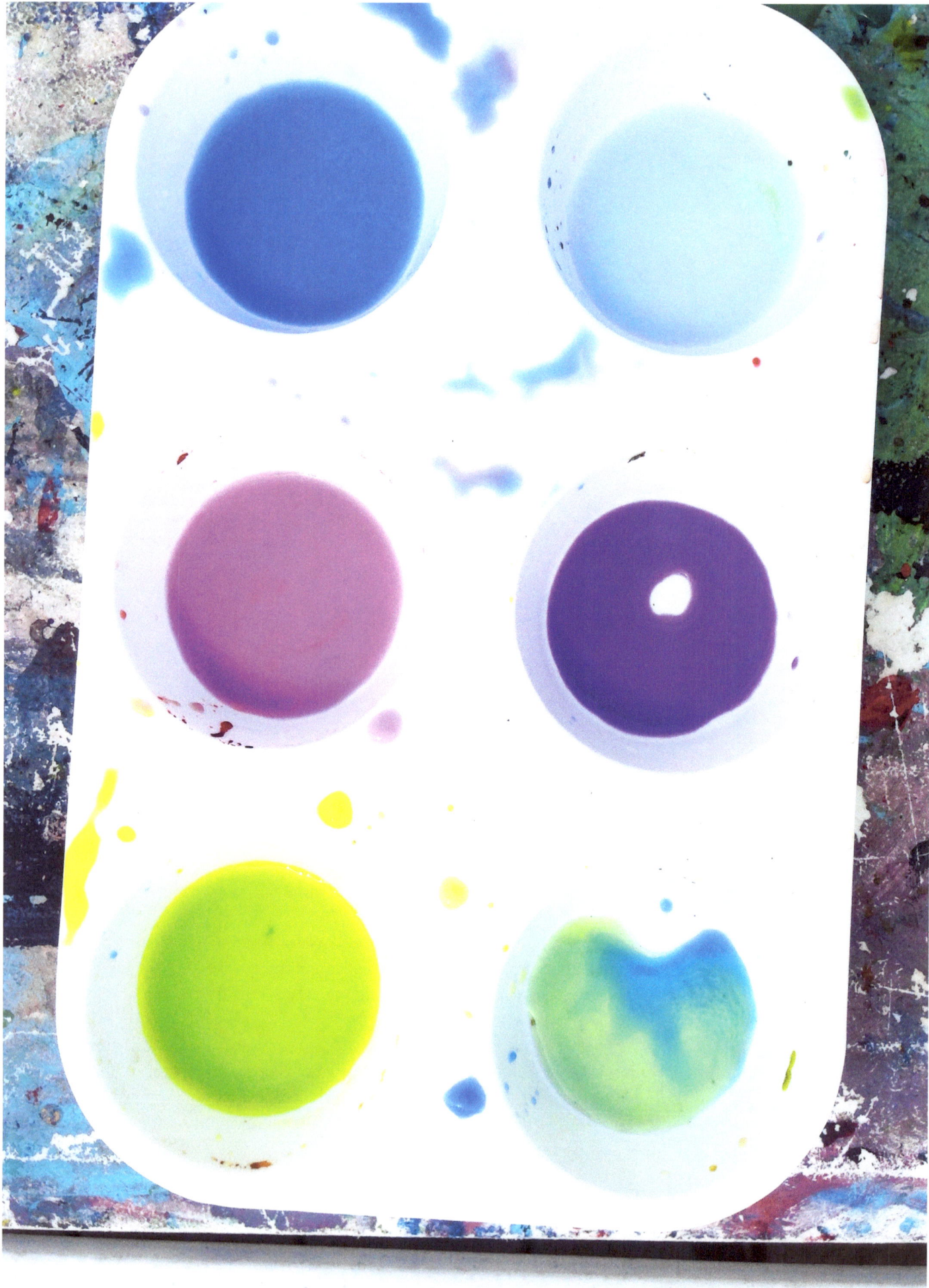

Chapter 8.

Paints Best for Color Mixing

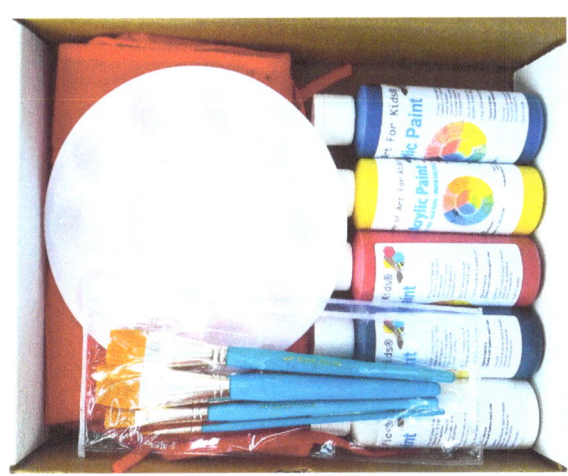

In my opinion, these are the best paints to use for color mixing, because they can all be diluted translucent, which reflects lots of light. All of these paints dilute with just water. They are also all water-soluble and do not require any artist paint thinners, solvents, or chemicals. These paints come in student grade and non-toxic. Do not use adult grade products for children under the age of 12 years. Always look to see if there is a "Conforms to ASTM D-4236" label somewhere on the bottle. "Conforms to ASTM D-4236" means the paints are not hazardous and are safe for kids to handle.

Watercolor
Acrylic
Guache
Dry watercolor pan cakes
Watercolor pencils
Watercolor crayons
Watercolor

Watercolor is considered fine artist paint and is traditionally painted on thick watercolor paper. Watercolor's texture is watery and clear but rich in pigmentation. Watercolor dilutes easily. Watercolor dries transparent and you can usually see through the pigment. Watercolor has pigments with minimal binders and dries smooth and flat leaving no coating or film behind. It has no sticking power, but can be absorbed by paper surfaces. Watercolor paints go a long way with coverage using only a small amount. Commercially, watercolor paint comes in bottles, tubes, and dry cakes.

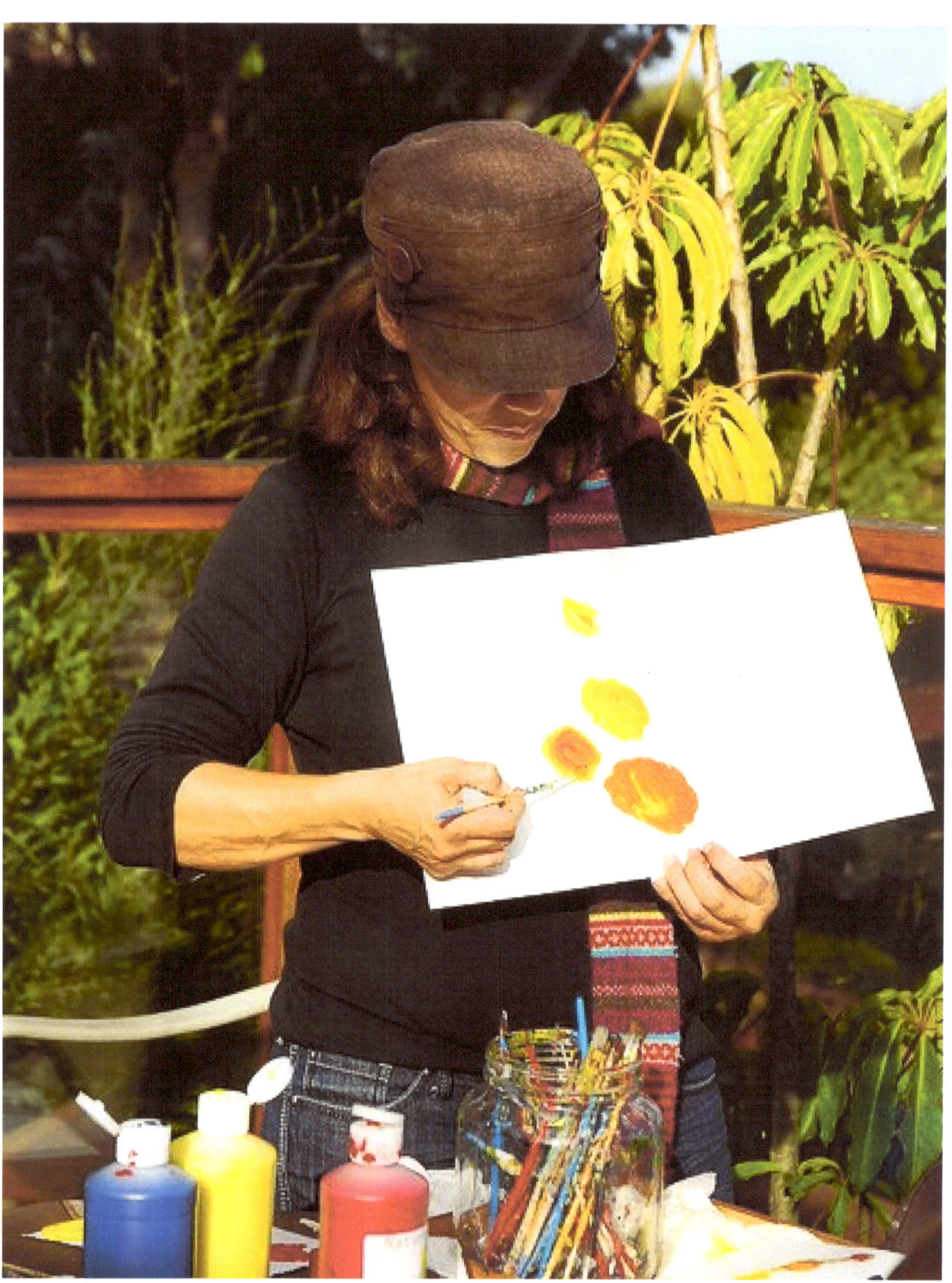

Acrylic

Acrylic paints are ideal for teaching advanced color theory because the proper primary colors are available in acrylic. Acrylic is considered fine artist paint and is traditionally used on a canvas. Acrylic is made with pigments and binders that help stick to a canvas and most surfaces. This special resin binder is thick and creamy and becomes water-resistant when dry. When it's dry, it almost has a plastic finish because the resin is made out of polymer. Acrylic paint is a fast drying paint. The finish dries matte, semi-glossy, or glossy, depending on the grade you purchase. Acrylic is water-soluble and dilutes well with water, which is how you thin this paint out. No toxic paint thinners are needed to dilute acrylic. Commercially, acrylic paint comes in bottles and tubes.

Guache

Gouache paint is similar to watercolor, but does not dry transparent. Gouache dries solid, also known as opaque, which has better hiding power. You will not be able to see the paper through the paint like you can with watercolor paint. The texture of gouache is thick out of the tube, and can be thinned with water. No coating or film is left behind. Gouache dries smooth and flat. Commercially, it comes in tubes. Tubes are generally smaller than acrylic.

Dry Watercolor Pan Cakes

Similar to watercolor paints, these are just dry watercolors in a round cake shape. When watercolor cakes are wet, they have the same effect as basic watercolor. Watercolor cakes are dry pigments that can come in either a plastic or metal pan. They are good for working on smaller artworks, easy to store, and much more portable for outdoor use. There is no need for a palette or squeezing tubes of bottles out. Kids can work directly from a pan without having to use a palette.

Watercolor Pencils

Watercolor pencils work just like traditional colored pencils, but can also be used to mix colors. Watercolor pencils are water-soluble, so when a child brushes over them with a wet paintbrush, the pigments dissolve and become translucent like watercolor paints.

Watercolor Crayons

Watercolor crayons are a water-soluble product that dissolve when water is washed over them, unlike a regular crayon. They can also work great for mixing primaries into secondaries. These crayons have bright pigment concentration and are similar to the texture of oil pastels.

Translucent

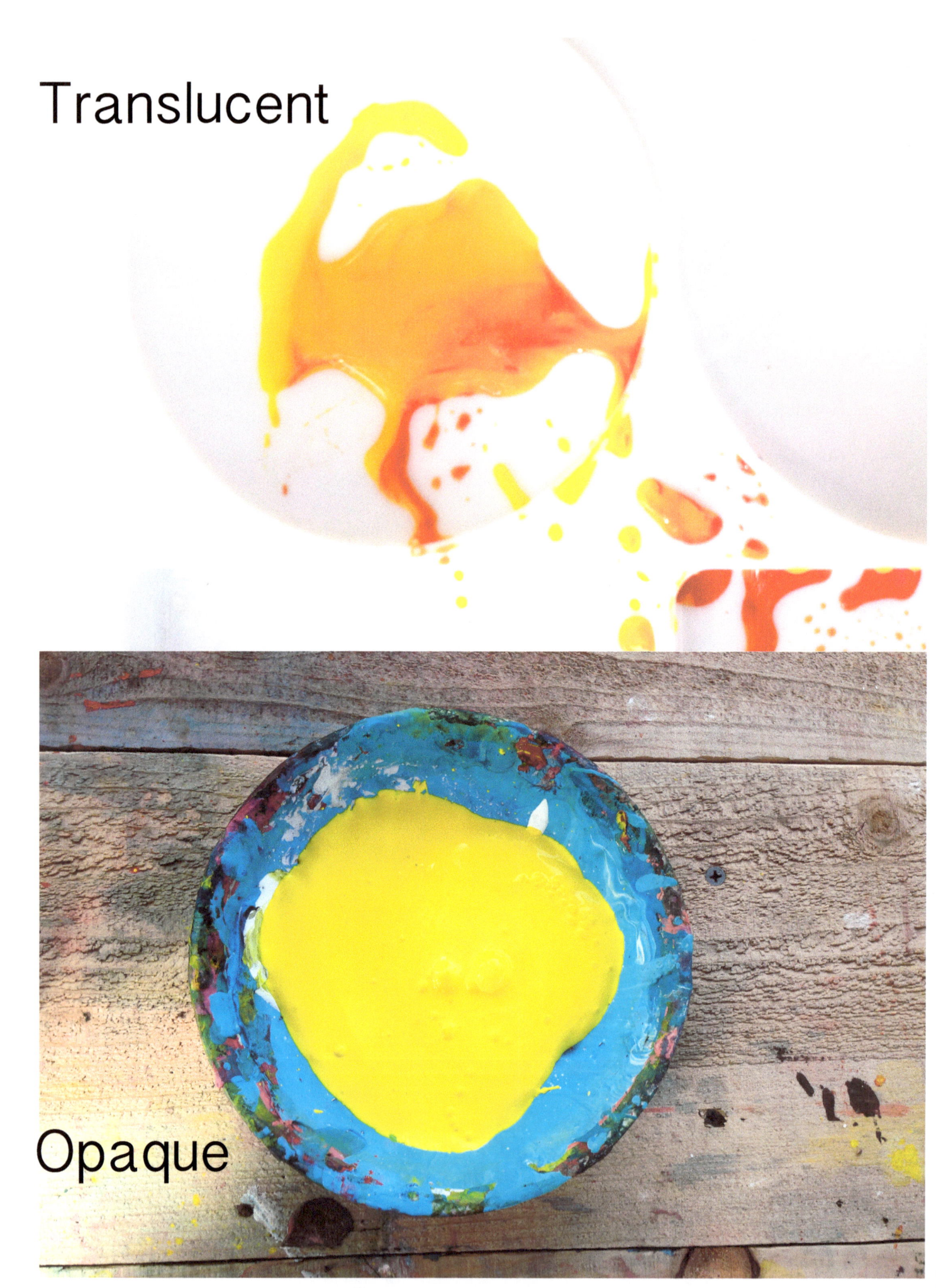

Opaque

Chapter 9.

Translucent vs. Opaque Paint

Some paints are clear and see-through while other paints are solid and you can't see through them. This is the difference between translucent and opaque paint.

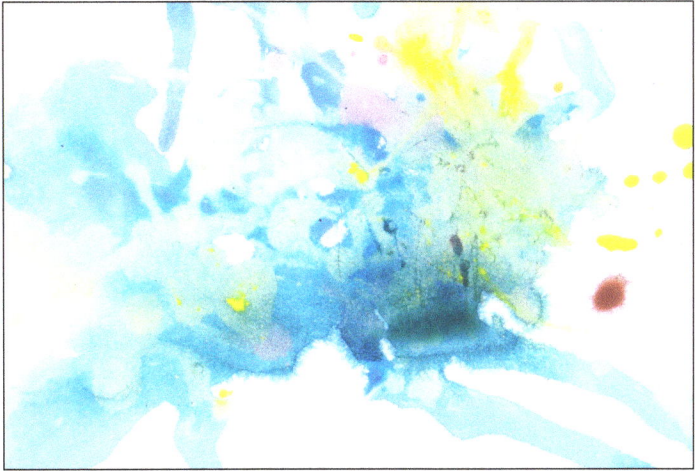

Translucent

Translucent colors do not have any fillers, binders, or solid blocking pigments. This makes the paint look watery and clear, showing only the pure pigments. This also makes the paper visible through the color when dry. You can usually see the paper right through translucent paint.

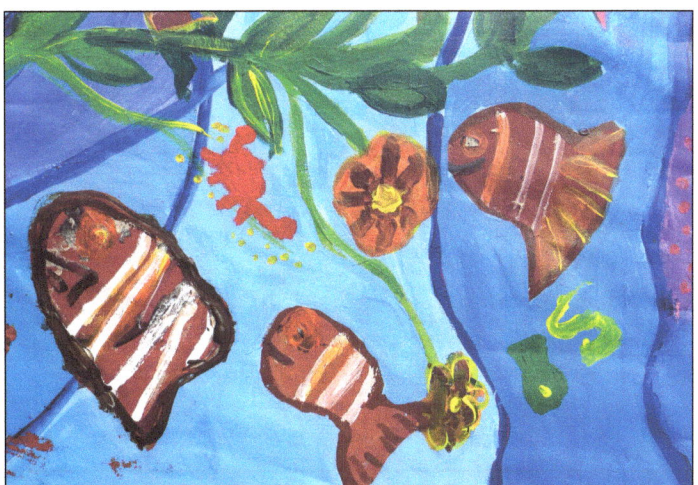

Opaque

Opaque paint obscures the eye from seeing through its layers. Most opaque paint is filled with white (titanium dioxide), blocking earth pigments, or fillers like kaolin clay. You will not be able to see the paper through opaque paint; you will only be able to see the solid color of the paint. Your surface will have a solid cover of opaque paint.

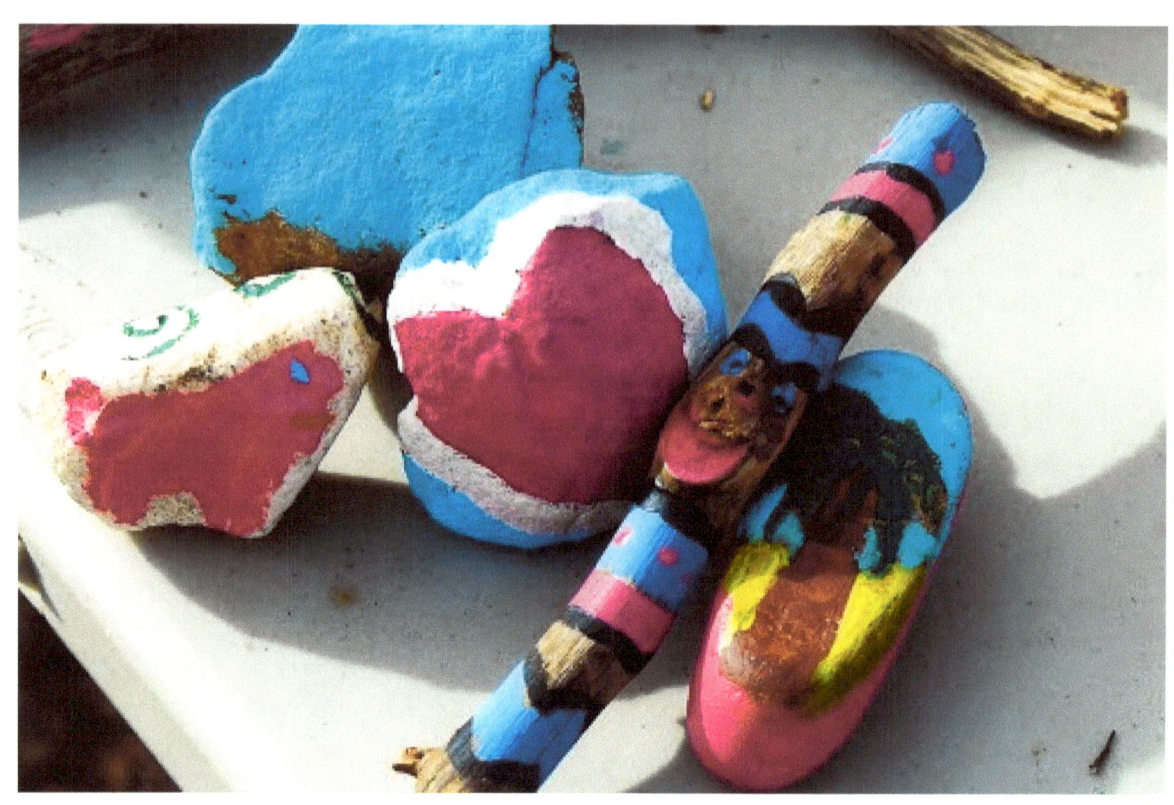

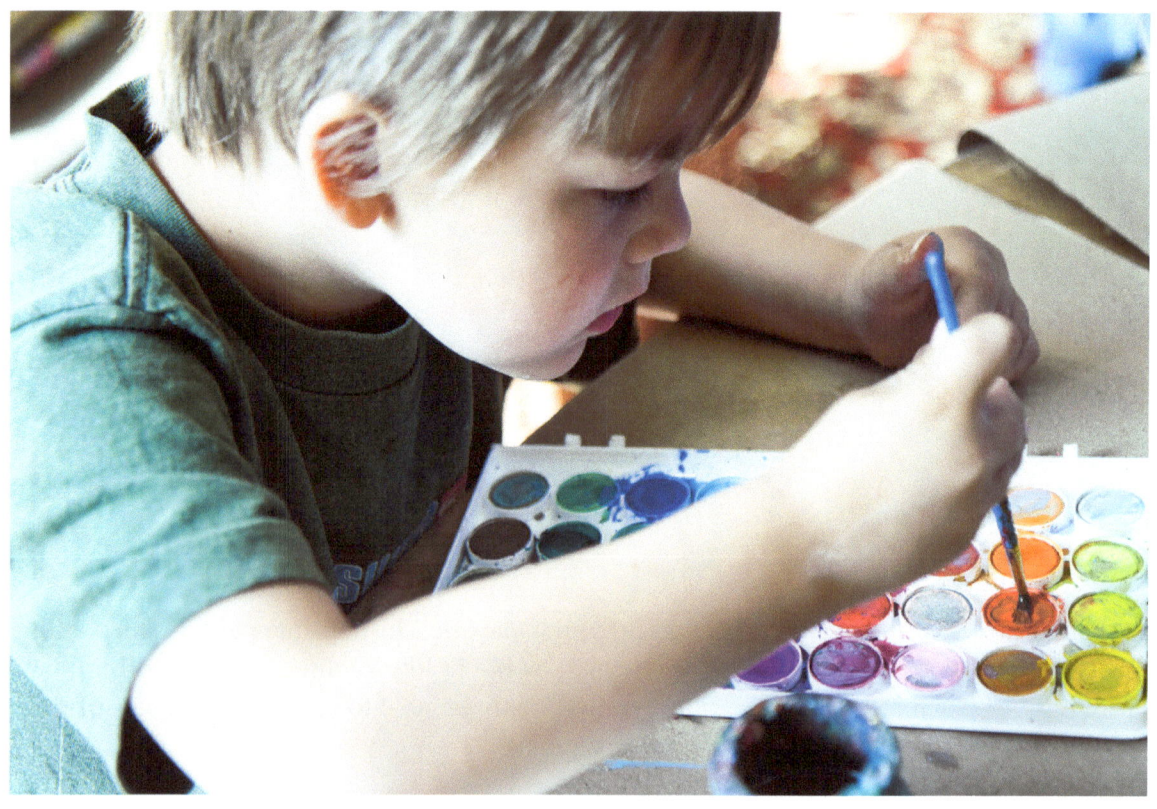

Chapter 10.

Other Colors, Besides Primaries

Ready-Made Colors

Ready-made paints are ready to use and no color mixing is required. These paints are mixed and ready like paints you choose from a hardware store for painting walls. You can pick a variety of ready-made colors at any art supply store. A good selection to have around for projects outside of primary color mixing can be a typical rainbow set of colors: red, orange, yellow, green, blue, and purple, plus black, white, brown, and pink to get started with.

Rainbow Color Swatch

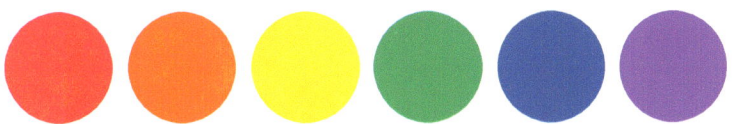 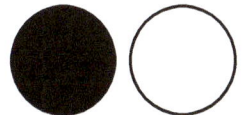

Ready-Made Color Swatch Examples

Here is a list of colors to have on hand for typical paint projects and mixing. Having a basic set of primary colors is good; kids can always mix all your secondary colors like green, orange, and purple. Black and white help with mixing shades, tints, and tones. Having this selection of colors gives you all the necessary colors you need for other fun painting projects or mixing primaries into secondaries.

Primary Colors: Red, Yellow, Blue
Black & White
Ready-Made Colors: Teal Blue, Purple, Yellow, Pink, Skin tone, Orange, Green, Gold, or Silver. Get these in neon, pastel, or bright colors.

Ready-Made Color Swatch

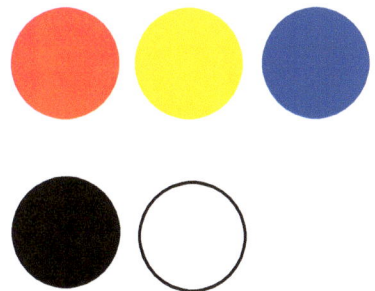 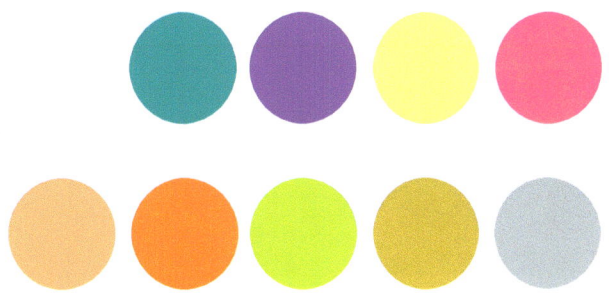

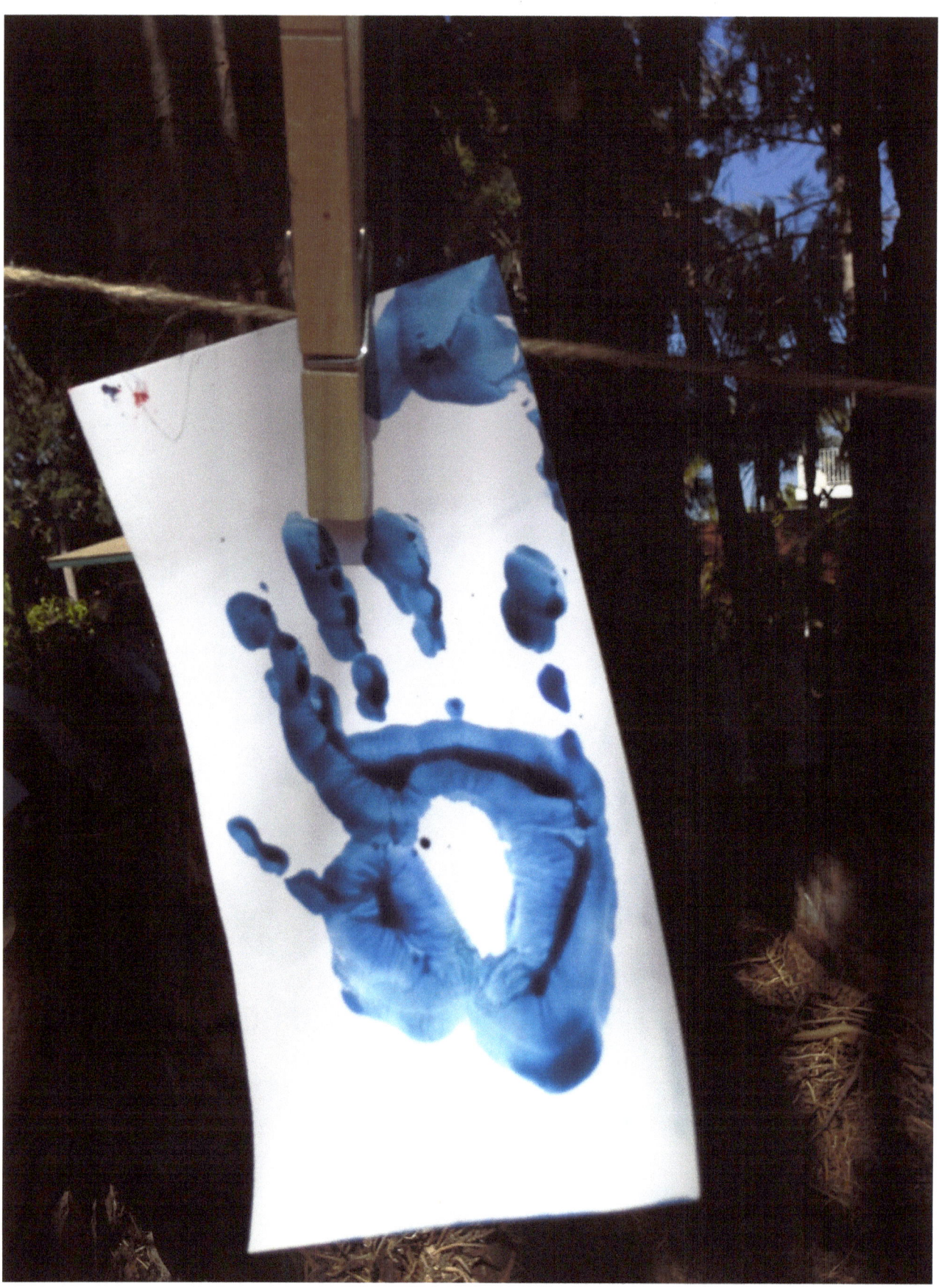

Chapter 11.

Beware of Dark Pigments
Making aGray Mass

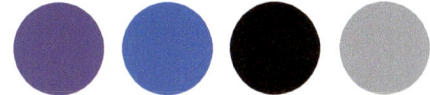

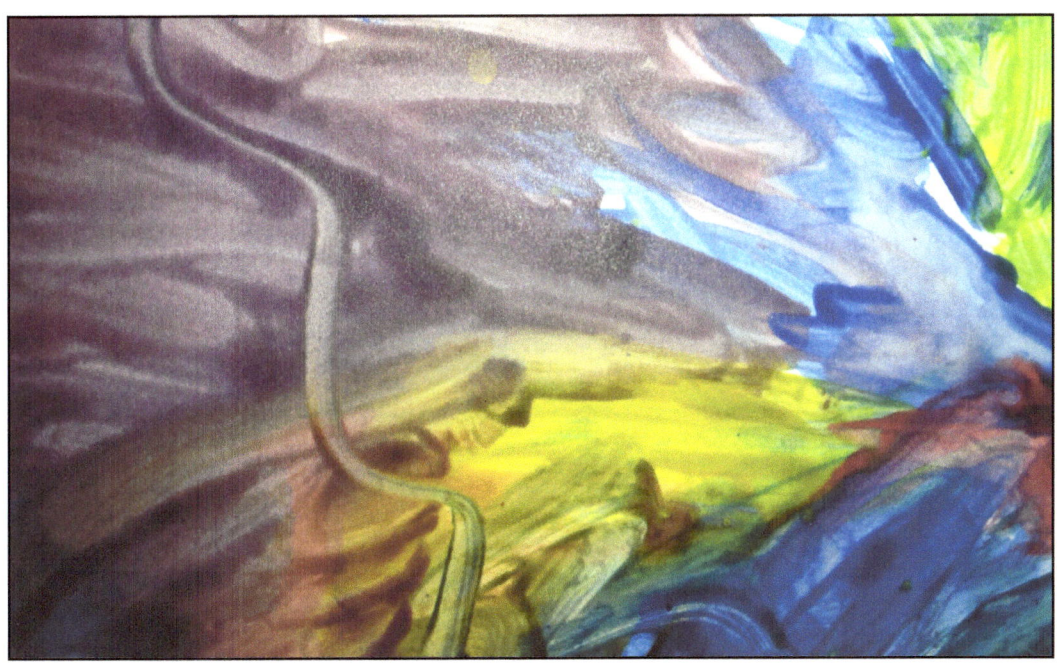

I have spoken to hundreds of teachers and parents who expressed frustration at how most young kids' paintings turn into a gray mass of colors at the end of painting. My explanation is this: Young kids lack the experience and understanding of how dark pigments are strong and can change light pigments. It's not until kids have lots of experience with dark colors that they understand how to control this.

My solution is to limit too many dark pigments in the young painter's palette until they truly understand how dark pigments overpower light colors. I usually limit dark pigments from 15 months to five years until more controlled fine motor skills take place.

Black does teach important lessons on how to mix different shades in advanced painting. Black is the darkest pigment besides blue and violet. Lots of mixing with the dark colors like black, dark blue, dark greens, and violet shows kids how strong dark pigments change their lighter pigments with little effort. Controlled mixing like this takes years of practice. There comes a time when kids understand how to control dark pigments in their palette with ease after lots of mixing experiments.

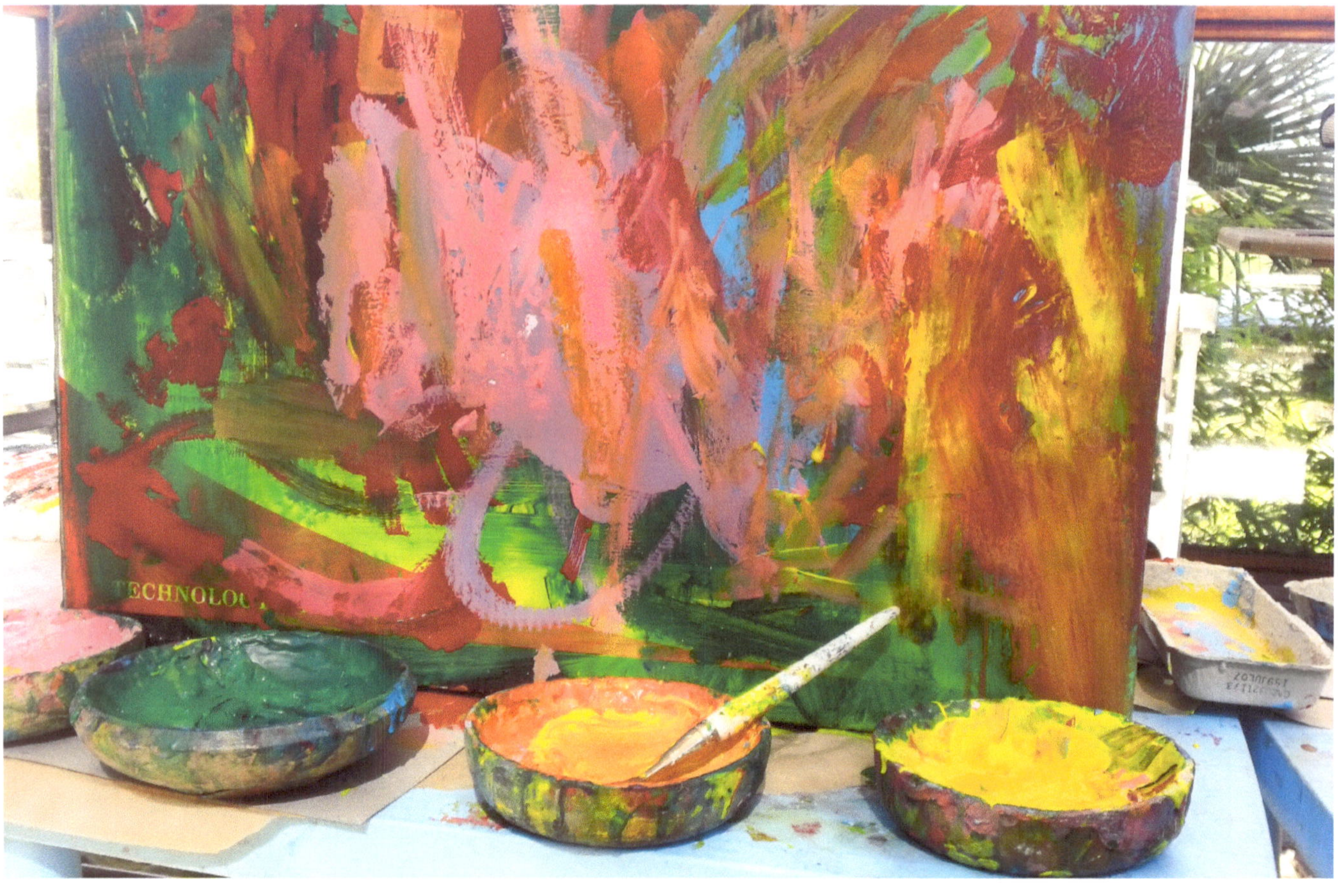

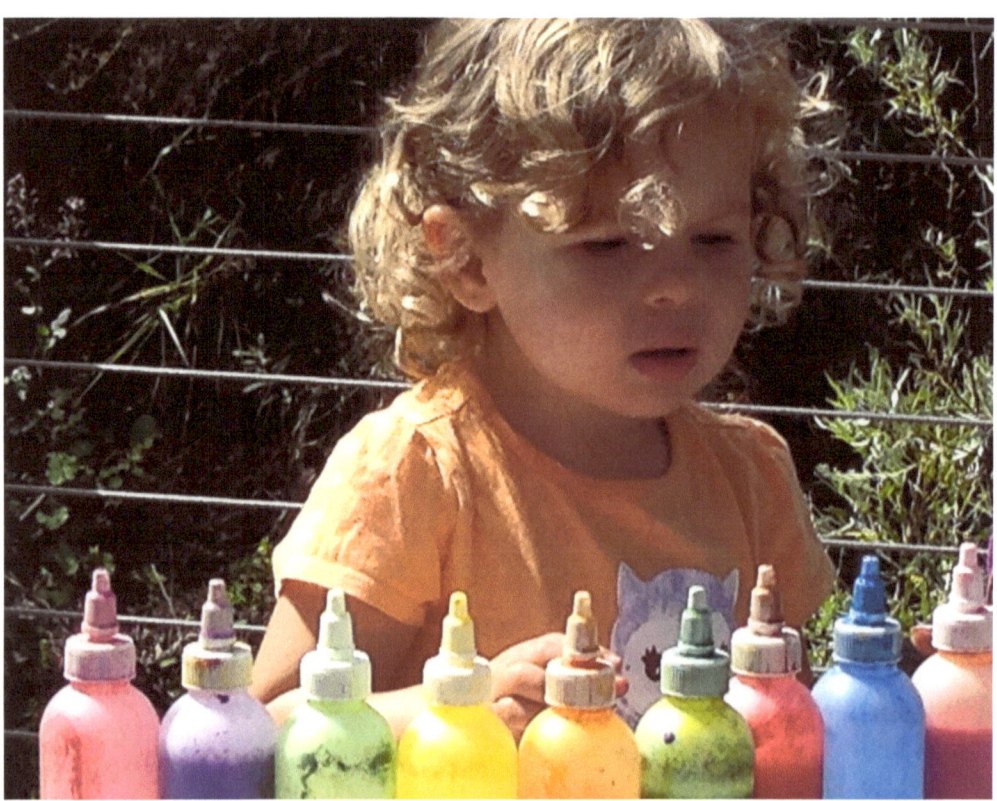

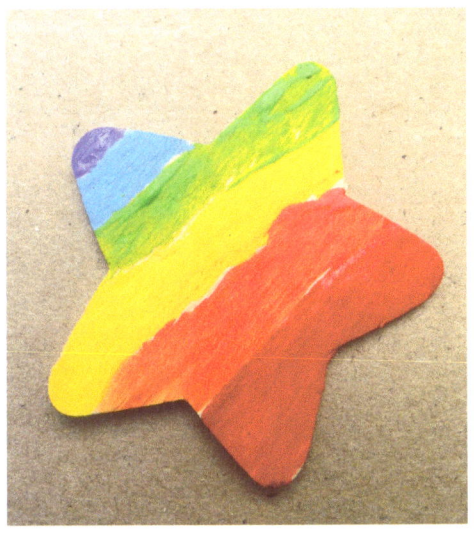

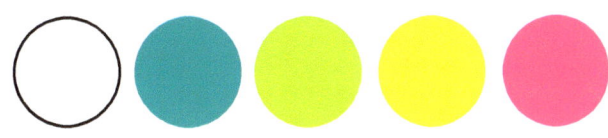

Tip!

Light Pigments

Having fewer dark choices always works best when working with young kids. Toddlers are just learning how to mix and keep colors inside their palettes. Add larger amounts of light pigments for young kids. This type of setup will help them learn fine motor control. As they grow and get more refined with using a paintbrush, you can add smaller amounts of paints and more darker color choices.

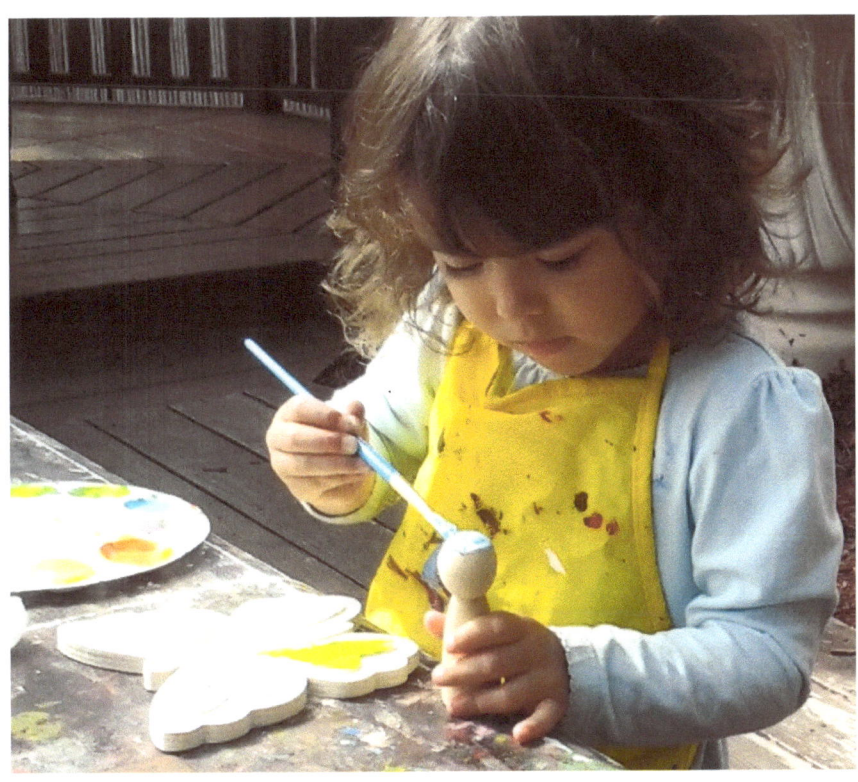

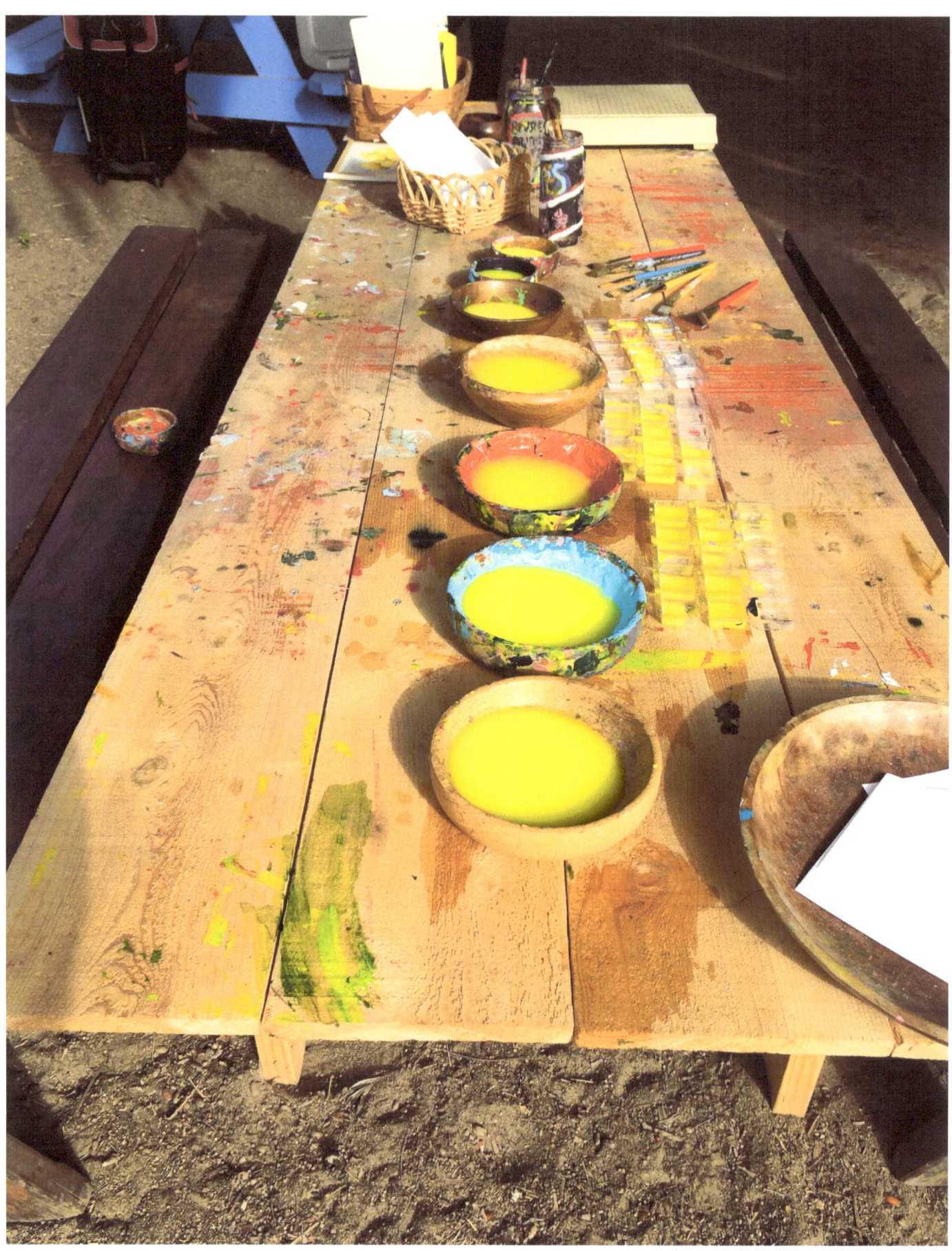

Chapter 12.

Materials and Set-up

This materials list and set-up is designed for kids, not advanced artists. Observing children over the years, I've noticed the fine-motor struggles kids commonly face while learning to mix colors and create painted artworks in the beginning years. This materials list and set-up helps kids through all their developmental gross to fine-motor art phases.

Watercolor Paper/Paper
Paints
Smock
Palette
Paintbrushes
Wash Jar
Napkins
Baby Wipes
Glass Droppers
Squeeze Bottles
Water Tub Dipping and Pouring
Trays
Art Space For Mixing
Lighting for Mixing
No Art Easels
Drying Kids' Lesson Projects

I recommend all color mixing be done on thick white paper that can absorb paints well. Watercolor paper is my first choice. Kids can use other thick papers and boards if you can't get watercolor paper. Offer small pieces of paper to explore color mixing combinations. This allows kids to do lots of mixing experiments. Remember, young kids need lots of practice, which can go through lots of paper. This is why I recommend smaller pieces. All the paints listed work well on watercolor paper.

Smock

Mixing color can be a messy activity that usually gets on clothes. Planning ahead for these types of messes can provide hours of creative fun and give parents and teachers peace of mind. Always have children wear clothing they can get messy in while mixing colors. Similar to play clothes, your child should have art clothes. It's also helpful if you wear clothes that can get messy because you will get very close to these paints while helping. Kids can cover up with a smock or old shirt. Smocks are similar to a cooking apron.

Palette

A palette has two functions, a place to hold paints so you can load your paintbrush and a place in which to mix paint colors. Palettes come in many shapes; some are plastic, metal, or porcelain. For beginner painters, I

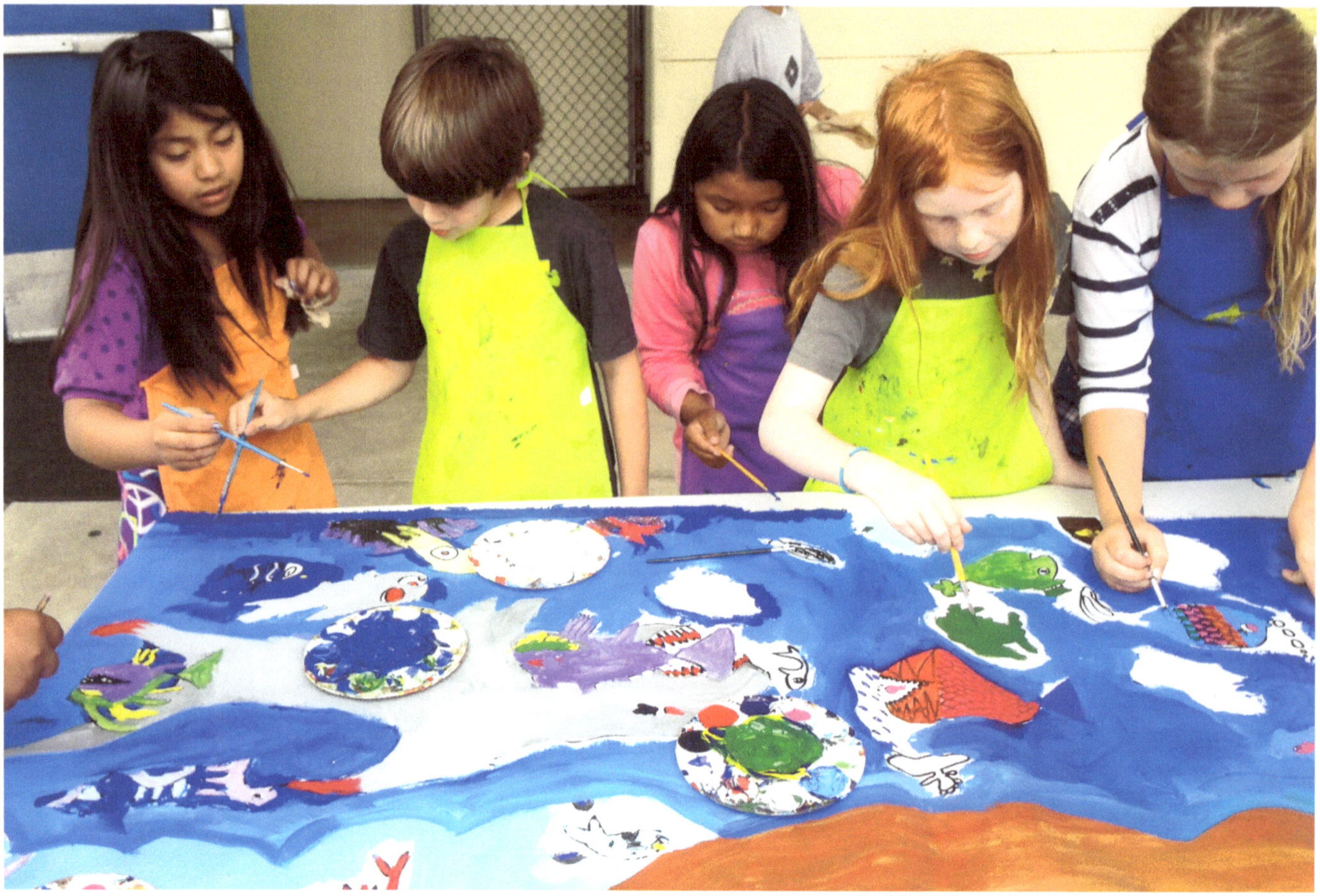

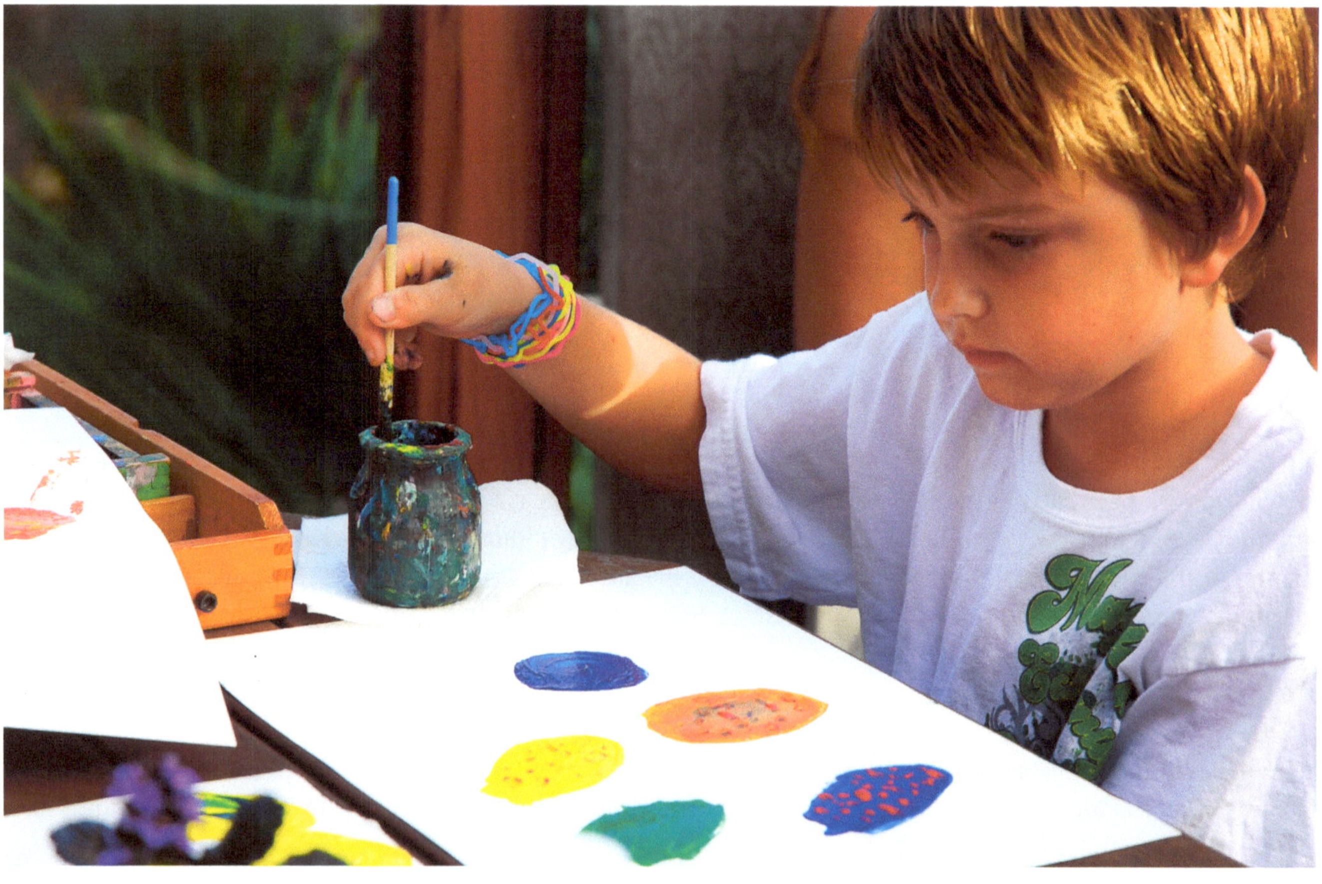

highly recommend a white plastic palette. Some palettes are flat and some have dips in them called wells. Some wells are round or square, and any shape will do for kids. I don't recommend flat palettes for beginning painters. Try to get a palette with wells. This will help kids keep from spreading paint around their workspace and into other colors. Beginning painters will learn to dip their paintbrushes only in the designated wells holding specific colors.

If a palette is not an option, you can use a paper type palette like a paper plate or egg carton and even a thick piece of cardboard. You can dispose of paper palettes into the trash when you're all done. A paper palette works best with thicker paints.

Thinner, watery paints should be in a deep well palette or bowl. The function of a palette is similar to a plate, a place to hold messy foods; if your food is runny, then you usually uses a deep bowl. The more watery the paint is, the deeper the wells should be. You can also use deep small bowls or containers for kids to paint from. Do not use your kitchen dishes unless you are going to designate them for painting only. Never eat off dishes that held paints. Watercolor washes out well and acrylic peels off plastic palettes easily when it's all dried. When kids are learning to mix primary colors into secondary colors, this should all be done within a palette.

Paintbrushes

Following these paintbrush tips will make mixing enjoyable and easy for kids to learn quickly. Kids only need three paintbrushes, a large, a medium, and a tiny size. A large paintbrush is used for large areas; a medium size is to cover most common areas; and a very tiny brush is used to make small details. Each one of these paintbrushes should be easy to hold and no longer than seven to eight inches. Young children should not use adult length paintbrushes.

It's pretty common that you will need to replace paintbrushes from time to time, mostly because kids may forget to properly wash out acrylic or craft paints. Most acrylic and craft paints dry fast and harden like plastic due to the resin coatings inside them. There's no need to spend lots of money on paintbrushes; you should be able to find quality paintbrushes ranging from $1.00 to $5.00.

I recommend synthetic hair, not animal hair. Here are a few reasons why: Animal hair is costly for kids to take proper care of in the beginning years; secondly, animal hair falls out much more then synthetic hairs do and can show up on the surface of mixtures; and thirdly, synthetic hair washes out easier with warm soap and water. Young children should use a good quality paintbrush; resist using craft cheap paintbrushes with hairs that are not smooth and easy to paint details with. Good paintbrushes will cause less frustration than using poor brushes that don't allow kids to make smooth, natural brush strokes with ease.

Wash Jar

A wash jar is such an important part of mixing colors. Your painting set-up should never be without one. The wash jar is the container in which kids will wash out colors from their paintbrush. A wash jar helps kids keep their color mixtures pure. A wash jar keeps kids from walking around with a loaded, wet paintbrush trying to figure out how to clean it off. I recommend a glass jar you can see the water through. Your wash jar should be wide at the bottom, not narrow. The most common reason kids spill liquid is because containers are usually narrow at the bottom, so no narrow water cups or containers. Kids will be swishing a brush inside these jars so a heavy, wide bottom ensures no spills.

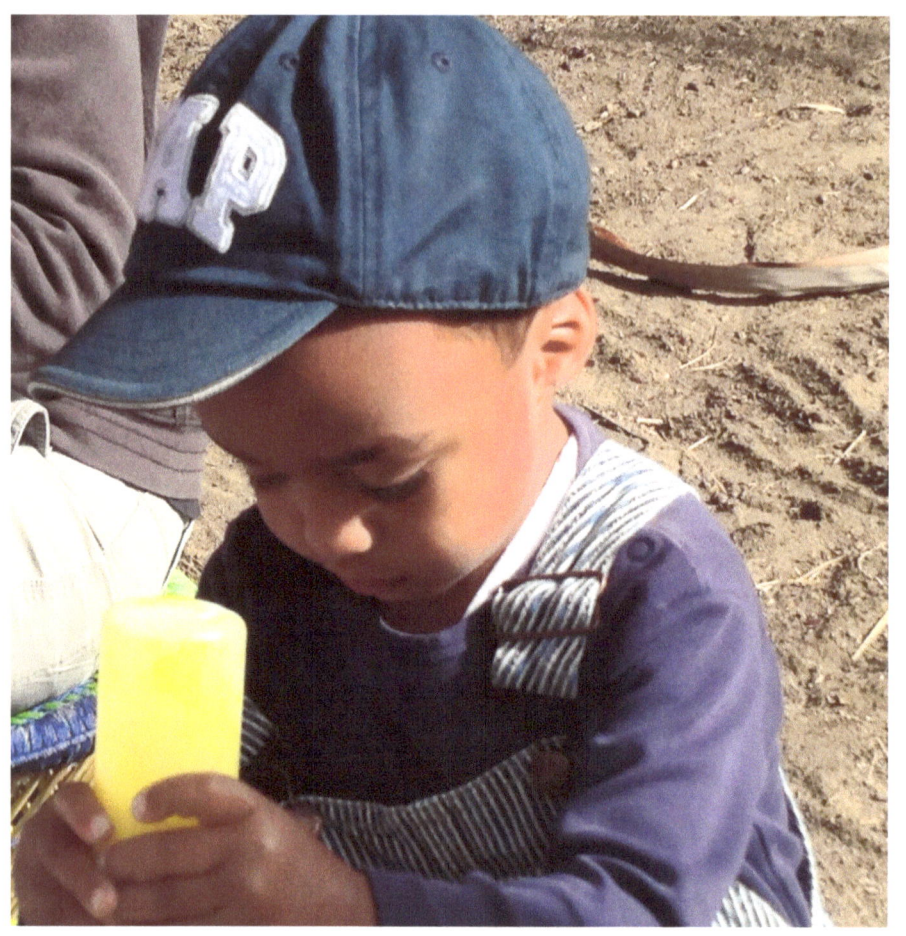

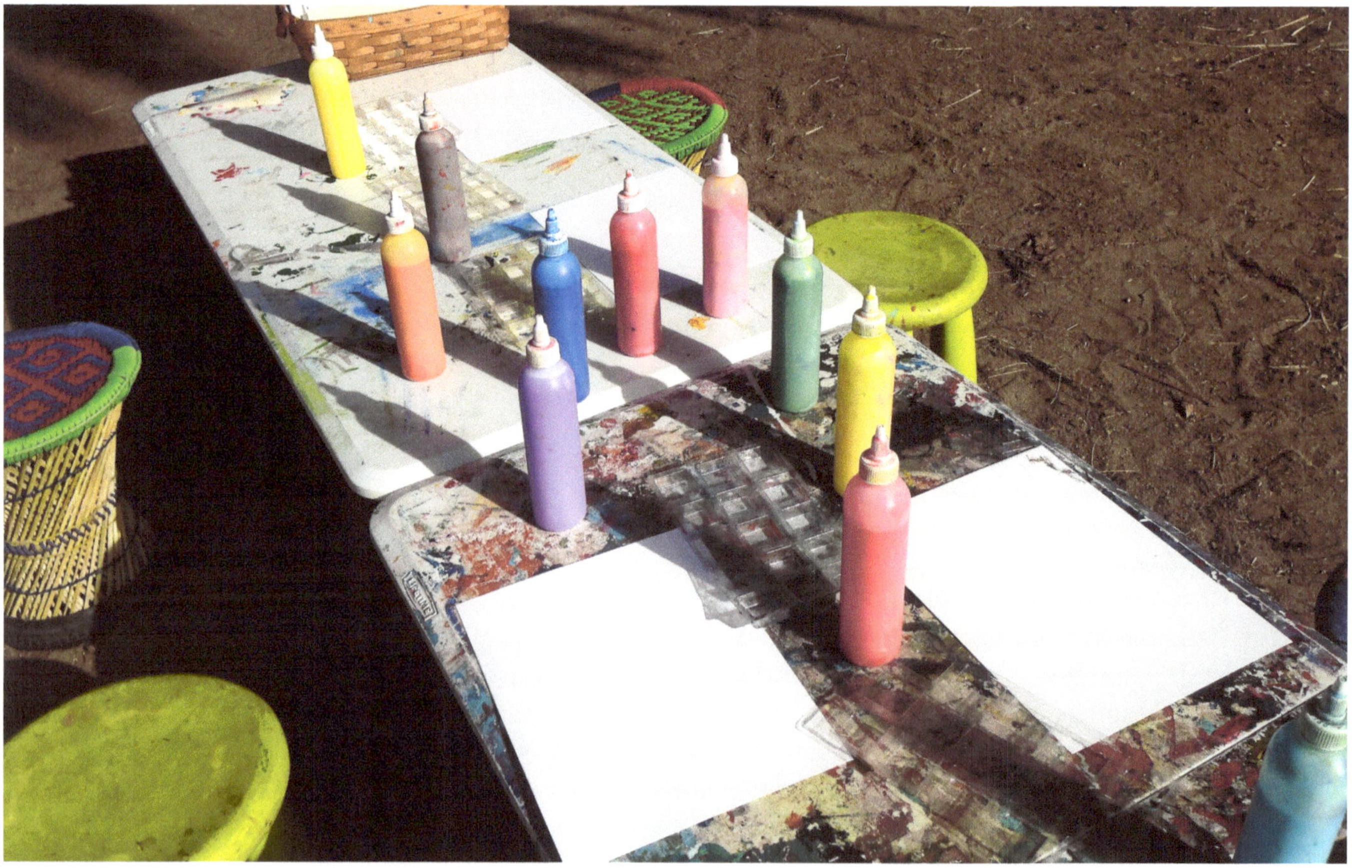

Depending on how long your child paints, they may need their jar refreshed from time to time with clean water. Generally, this happens if they started out with dark pigments and switched to a very light pigment. It may be hard for them to keep the light colors pure if they keep washing their brush in dark, murky water. This could keep pure secondaries from appearing properly. Refreshing their water helps with this frustrating aspect.

Assist young children not capable of safely carrying a glass jar across the room, and allow older children to do this task independently if they are capable and understand that paint pours into the trash or sink only without large splashes. Until a child refines his painting skills and equilibrium and a sense of gravity kicks in, a wash jar will work like a charm and reduce spills and messes.

Napkins

Napkins are another important element in keeping pigments from spreading around. The napkin in this set-up is for the paintbrushes only. Once a child washes the paintbrush in the washing jar, wiping it off on a napkin is the next step before dipping it back into the palette of colors. The napkin should be anchored under or near the washing jar. I always place it halfway under the jar so kids clearly understand this is where they wipe their paintbrushes off.

This napkin should not be used for wiping off hands. This is where the baby wipes come in. Be sure you explain to kids that the napkin is only for the paintbrushes and to leave it in its place so as to not spread paint around.

I don't recommend using rags or cloth for wiping brushes off. Rags are what traditional painters use while painting with acrylics and oil paints. However, a rag on the table will cause more mess than it will help clean up messes for kids. Rags are large and bulky for young kids and can actually cause paint to smear and drag paint around the table. With a napkin in place near the wash jar, this will not happen. Napkins may also need to be refreshed from time to time. Help young kids refresh their wash napkin until they are old enough to do this without spreading paint. Always keep a trashcan nearby to toss painted, soiled napkins in quickly.

Baby Wipes

Having baby wipes around can help when there is no washing station nearby. This also helps if you don't want kids moving around with paint on their hands. Baby wipes can be found in most grocery stores. I really like using baby wipes because they can safely wash off any water-soluble paint on hands. Wipes also work well for cleaning acrylic off of hands. Wipes have the right balance of mild soap and are not too messy to use. There is no water splash of paint that comes off them, and they absorb paint quickly. Of course, soap and water with a dry towel works fine. Just be sure your towel is okay to get paint on permanently. Like paint clothes, you can have paint towels or rags for drying hands and paintbrushes.

*Note

Try to explain to children before color mixing lessons that hands will get paint on them and this is part of the process of color mixing. Teach kids not to run back and forth trying to keep paint off their hands. Teach kids how to use their smocks and nearby wipes. Explain that messy hands are part of the process of mixing colors, and will happen here and there.

Glass Droppers

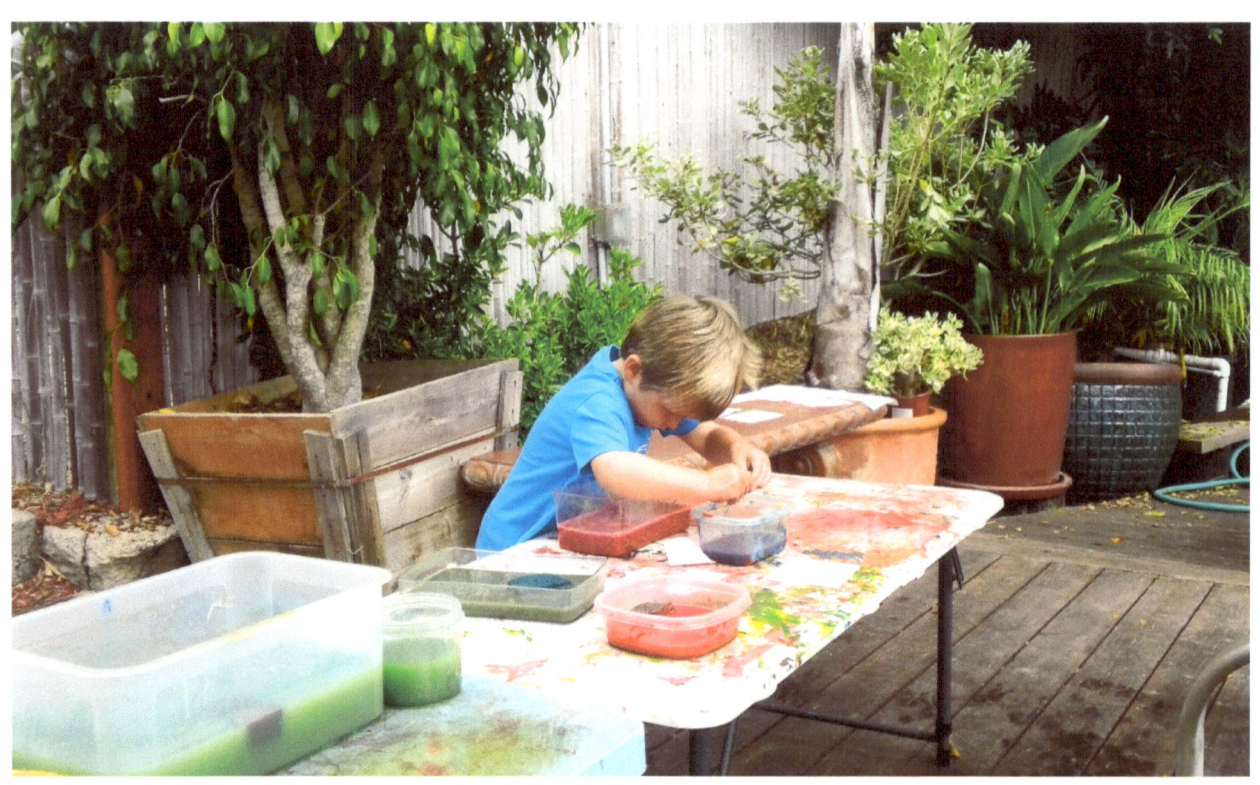

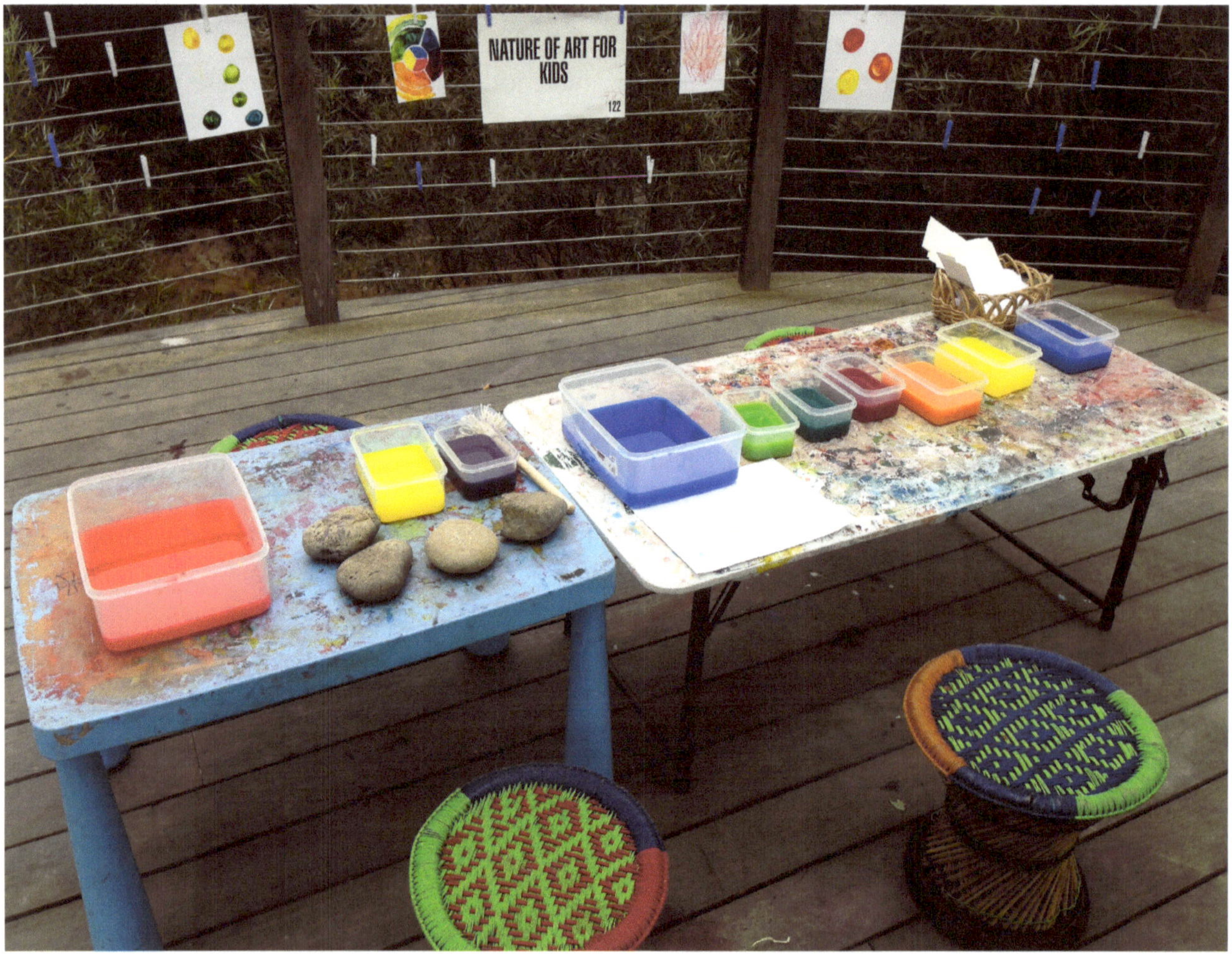

Using glass droppers is very exciting for kids. This turns color mixing into fun science color lab studying. I use droppers when I want kids to observe color changes and mixtures closely. All kids have to do is squeeze paints into other colors and see the colors change. Kids can use a paintbrush to mix up their drops into different hue values. Droppers can be used to teach most color theory lessons, which I find is a nice break

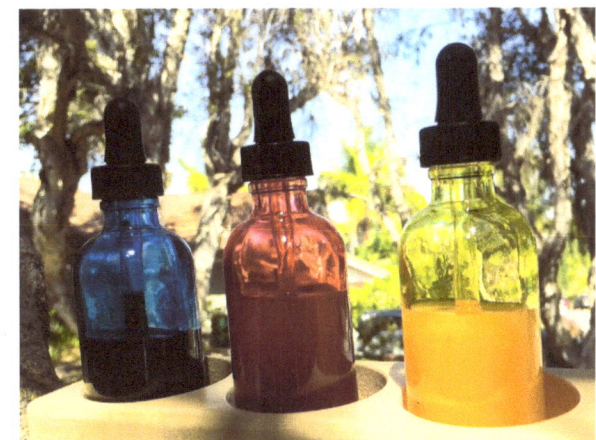

from using only a paintbrush. This works great when kids feel mixing ideas are difficult to understand. Once I show them how to drop colors into other colors, they get more relaxed about learning color mixing. Most of my students get carried away and can spend a good amount of time using these fun paint droppers. Paint droppers have a mad science feel about them! These droppers are very thick and I have never had any accidents with them. But, if you're working with just toddlers, I recommend using a plastic squeeze bottle, below.

Tip:

The key thing with mixing colors with a dropper is that kids can drop more or less of a color to see how to get different color values — to dark, darker, and darkest. They can observe how many more or less drops to use. It's easier to gauge with a dropper than with just a paintbrush. Since I created this new way of teaching color theory with droppers, it has been such a big hit in my classes.

Squeeze Bottle Painting

Similar to paint droppers, you can use any type of squeeze bottle for kids to drop colors on paper. I recommend this type of project be done outdoors with larger paper. Younger kids enjoy this tactile type of color play.

The best paints for squeeze bottle mixing are watercolor or very diluted pigments from acrylic. I prefer to use plastic squeeze bottles because I can adjust the stream of watercolor coming out. If the hole is too large, too much watercolor comes out, turning the activity into a "get wet activity." By adjusting the opening, a smaller amount of watercolor can be squeezed out. Young kids can look closely and see colors blend much better. A large gush of water does not allow kids to appreciate the colors or reflect on them. Most kids will get very wet, so dress for this mess.

Water Tub Color Play

Water tub color play evolved many years ago when introducing toddlers to primary color lessons. I noticed children getting transfixed on colors when pouring from bowl to bowl. They became delighted when colors transformed into another different hue. I even witnessed toddlers try to correct the colors by pouring other combinations of colors together. Toddlers were no longer distracted by their surroundings and became totally absorbed by these color transformations. I even noticed calming and relaxation set in. I knew they were not mixing colors intentionally, but they were processing discovery and they knew something was happening because of their actions.

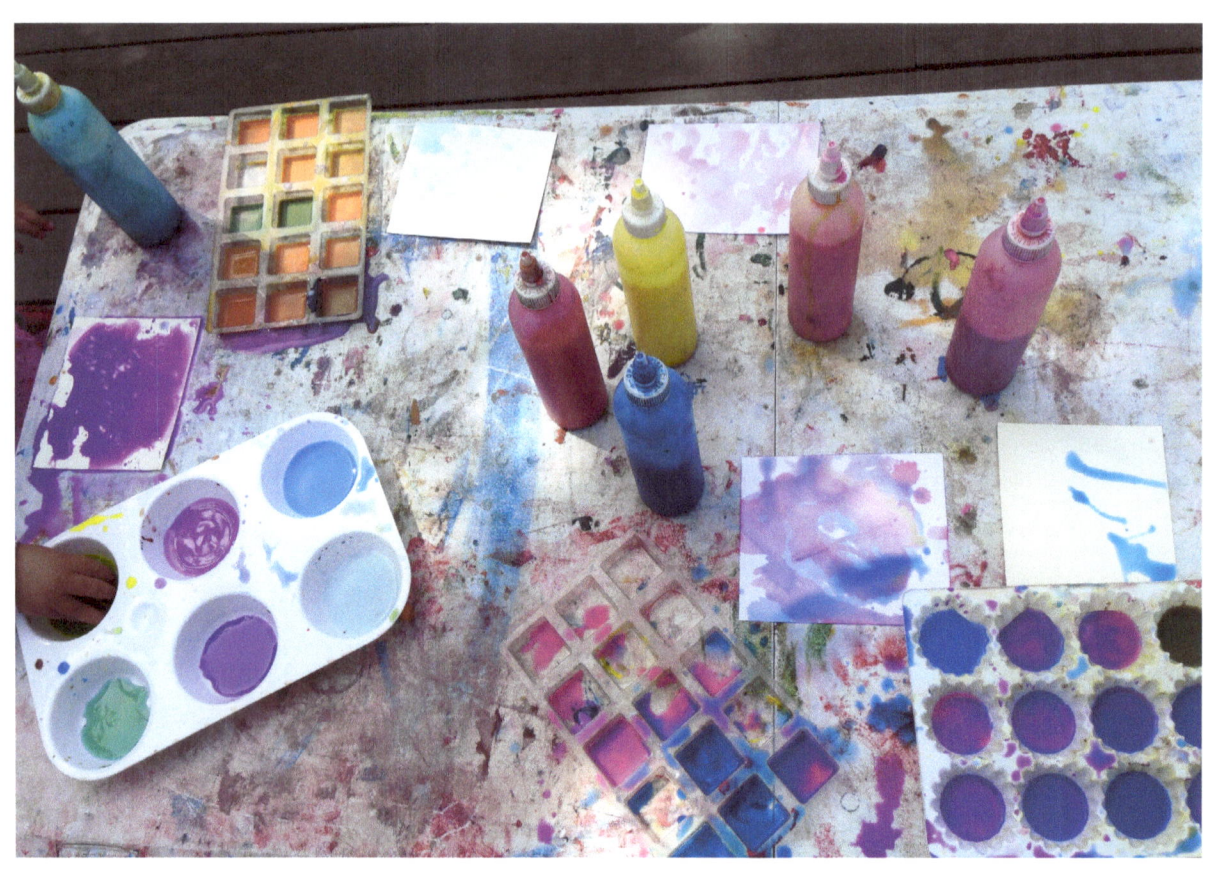

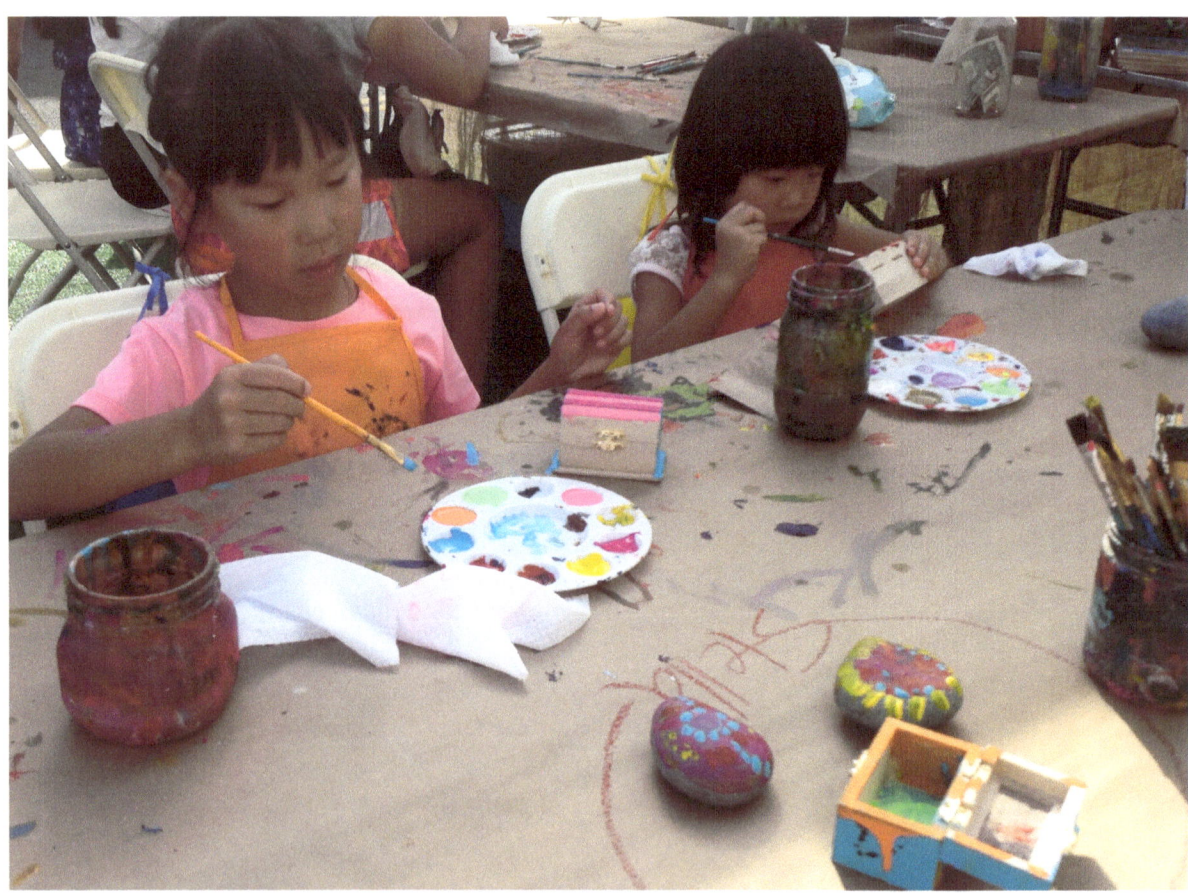

This set the stage for my squeeze bottle painting, water tub color play, and small tray color mixing lessons. I gave kids small papers to dip into these tubs to capture the colors they had a hand in mixing. Most kids get caught up in simple pouring activities. Later on, I added sponges and paintbrushes for the more fine-motor capable kids. Small trays and large palettes became part of my toddler materials for introducing color mixing play. I not only used primary colors, but also included ready-made, bright and fun colors in different sessions. It became the favorite for my youngest students. Older kids also love this process and enjoy the freedom to play with color this way.

The ratio for pigments is very light and watery. I fill a tub with water first, then add a drop of pigment and dilute completely, then add more pigment if I want a deeper color. This also makes watercolor paint washable and less likely to stain. Water play is messy, so I do this outdoors and have kids wear clothes they can get wet. This is great for early childhood process based art. Try to discourage kids from picking up large tubs to pour into each other; instead, give them tools like cups and smaller bowls to do that.

Palette Trays, Muffin Trays, and Ice Cube Trays

Palette trays have an effect similar to a palette with large wells. Kids like squeezing different colors into each well. You can use a basic palette or even an ice cube tray. This is great fine-motor practice. Toddlers aim and try to squeeze color drops into wells or ice cube trays, and it's so much fun!

Art Space for Mixing

This space can be created indoors or outdoors. The most important thing to remember is that making a space for art means creating space to get messy and have fun. An art space can support mixing projects and messes. An art space planned ahead of time should help kids enjoy mixing lessons. Everything should be to the child's body size to help them safely move around without getting injured.

A well-designed art space should have all these features in place before opening paints:

Table — Sturdy, flat surface to work on
Chair — Sturdy, safe chair at table level
Rug — Floor covering
Light source — Window or light nearby
Storage — Easy access for adults
Sink — Nearby

Lighting for Mixing

For children to create visual art projects, a good light source is important. I've spent many years observing children making artworks and understanding how visual perception is key to developing artistic skills. All art projects are colorful and need light to identify pigments and color hues. It's always a good idea for children to have a healthy light source to create in. Natural sunlight is the best, but a desk lamp can work just as well.

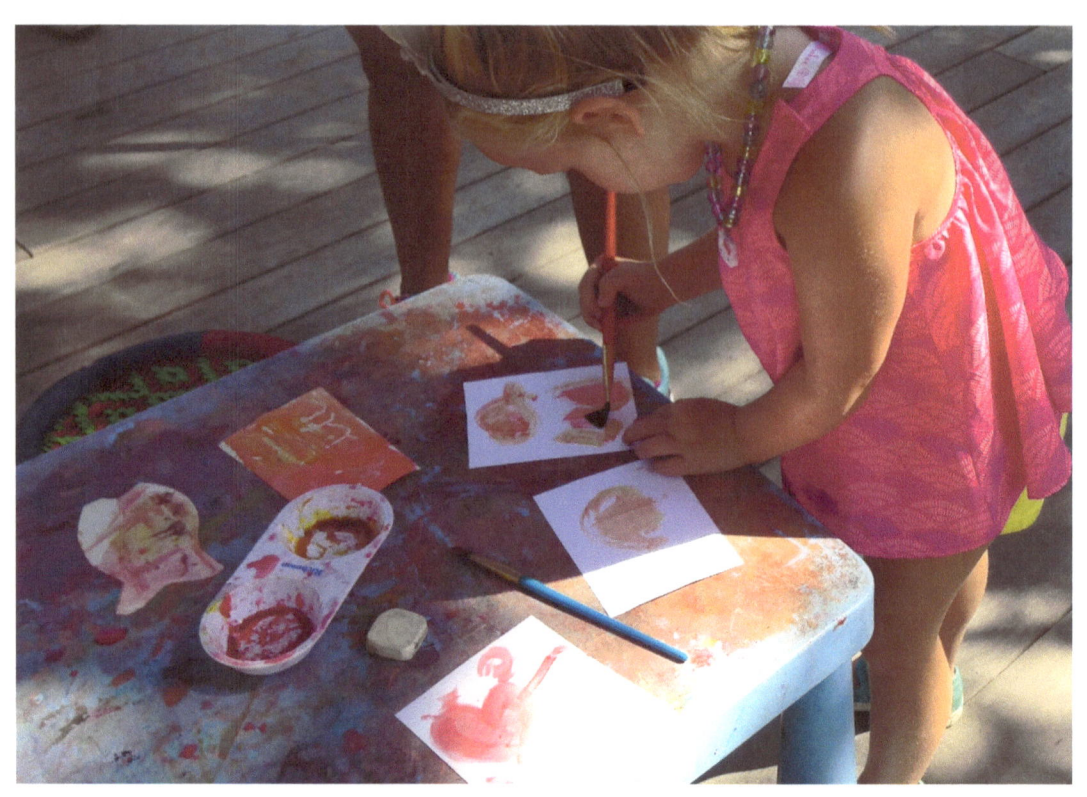

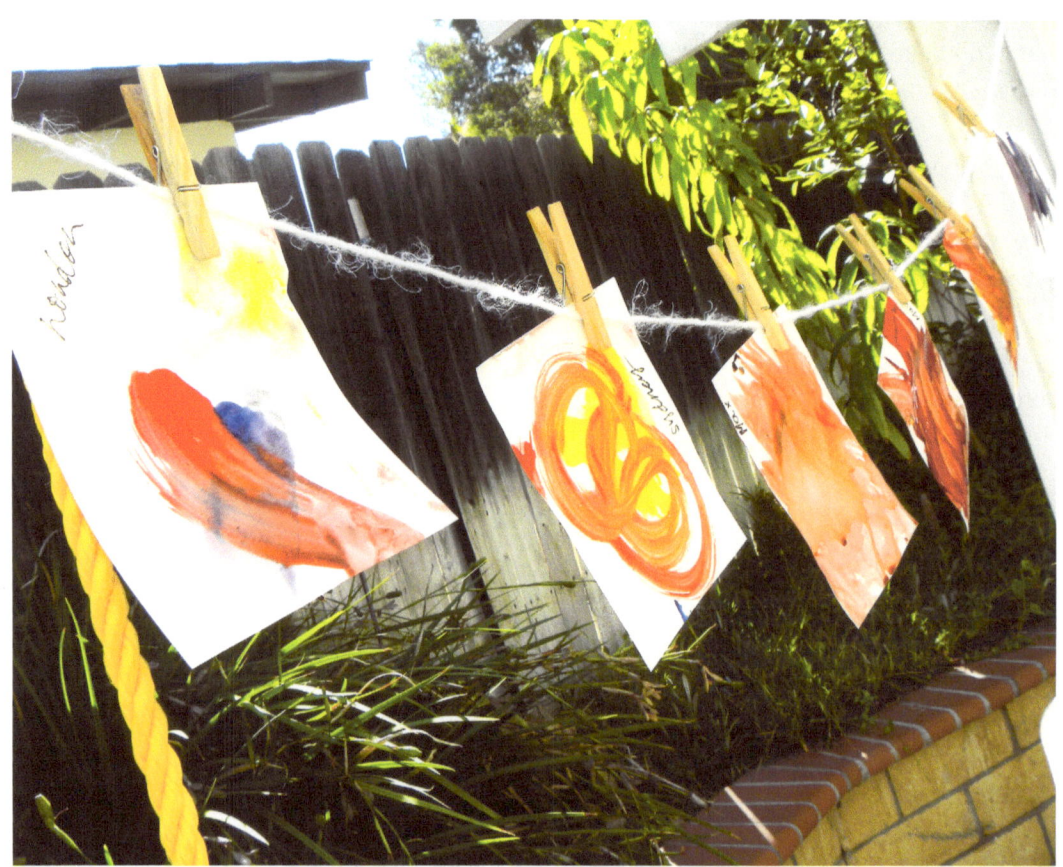

No Art Easels

My personal opinion on art easels is very different from most art instructors. I prefer not to teach young kids on easels. I use easels for older students over 12 years old. Younger children are not fine-motor capable of controlling paint drips or working on a slant until much later. I find it much easier and less frustrating for the child to learn color mixing lessons on a flat surface. Easels are fun for pinning up finished artworks.

Drying Kids' Mixing Projects

Over the years of teaching, I've devised ways for my students' paintings to dry without making extra mess or getting ruined, and to help them travel safely home from class. Almost everything kids mix up will need time to dry. Outdoor sunlight is the best and quickest way to dry projects. Paints in cooler temperatures take more time to dry. If you need to speed up the process of drying, then sunlight or a warm lamp over painted areas helps.

Some paintings will be moist and others will have thick paint and need extra time for drying. Acrylic is one of the faster drying paints and watercolor takes the longest to dry because papers are usually absorbed through from lots of water. Laying artworks flat is the best way for them to dry. If you are placing artworks outdoors to dry, you may want to add some weight in case a wind blows by. I use rocks found around landscapes as weights. Here are some ideas for a drying system or station:

Rocks — Outdoors, you can anchor lightweight paintings to keep them from blowing away.
Clothespin Line — You can hang and pin the paintings up on a line to dry.
Drying Racks — Drying racks can be found at teacher supply stores.
Deep Boxes — Place artworks inside wide cardboard boxes or box lids.
Open Shelves — Small to medium artworks can dry flat on an open shelf out of normal traffic areas.
Easels — Prop up lightweight to heavy artworks.
Outdoor Grass — You can lay large papers in the grass to dry.
Newsprint — Newsprint is good indoors where no wind will blow; lay projects down on newsprint to dry and discard newsprint when done or recycle for another project.

The important thing is to have a plan for where wet projects will dry before you open paints, and to show kids where to put wet projects to dry when they are done.

11 Color Mixing Lessons

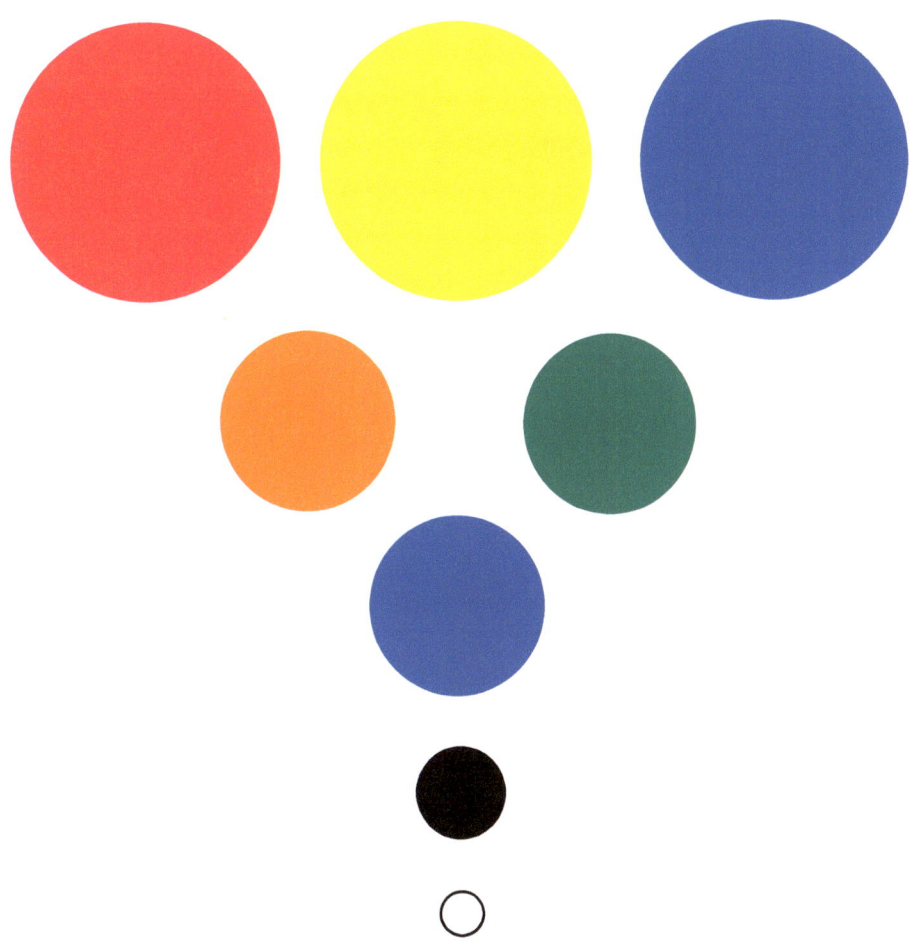

Lesson 1.

Have kids explore painting with these colors first, each in a separate lesson.
Kids can make light to dark washes in each primary.

Primary Colors

Lesson 1.   **Yellow**
Lesson 2.   **Red**
Lesson 3.   **Blue**

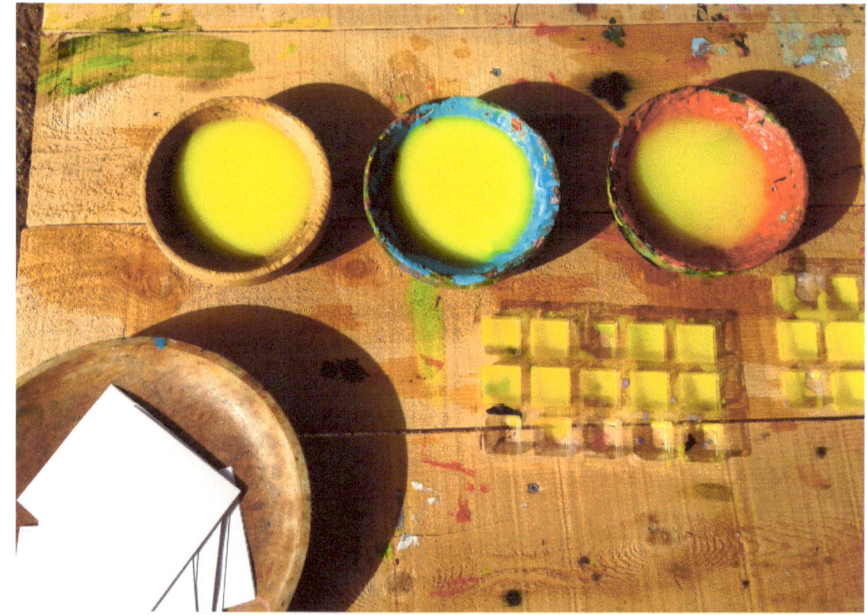

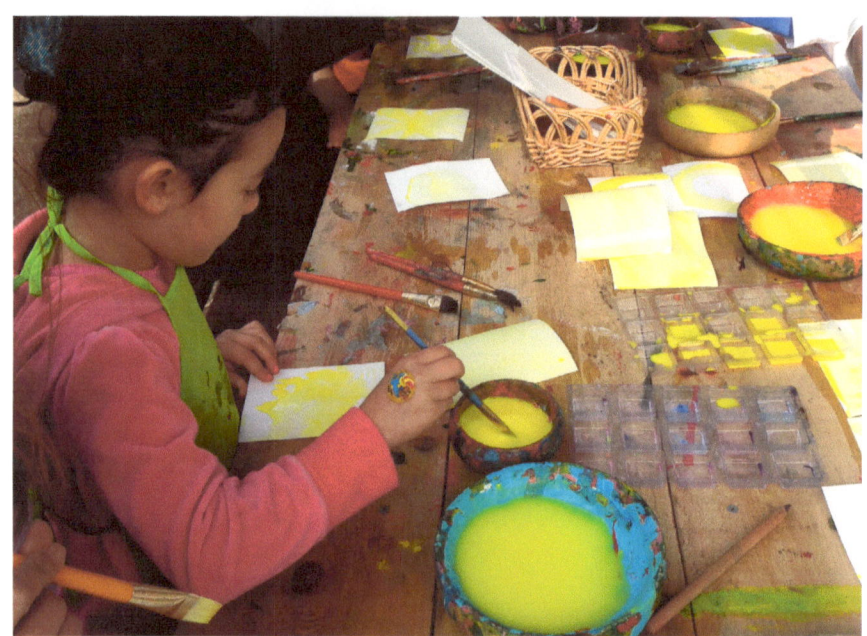

Lesson 2.

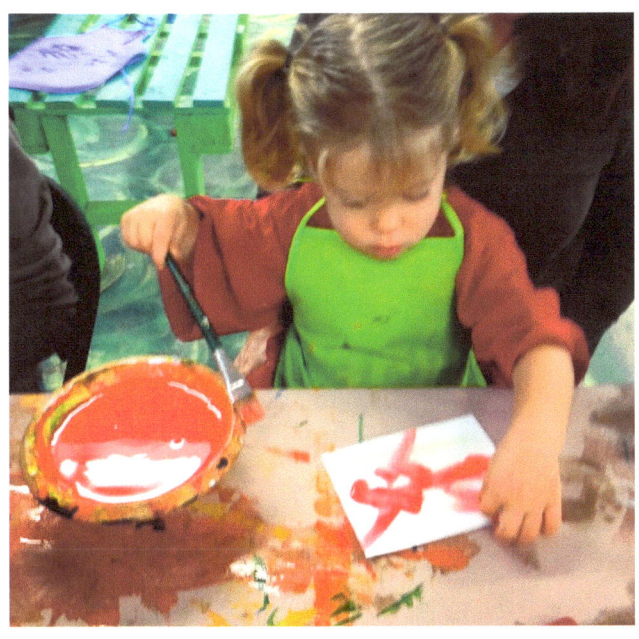

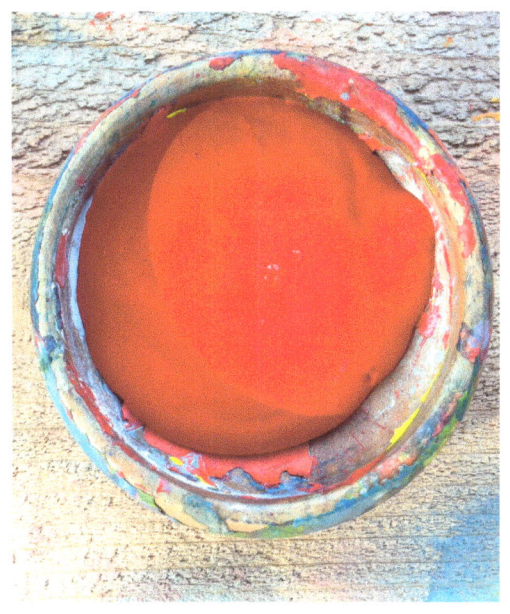

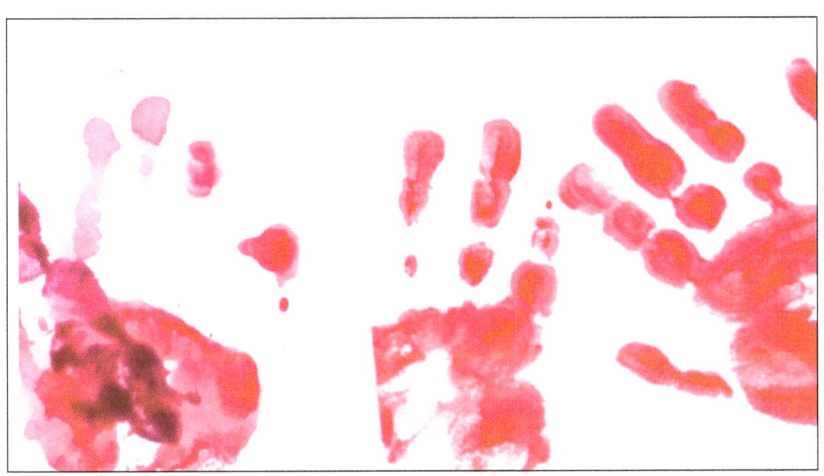

Lesson 3.

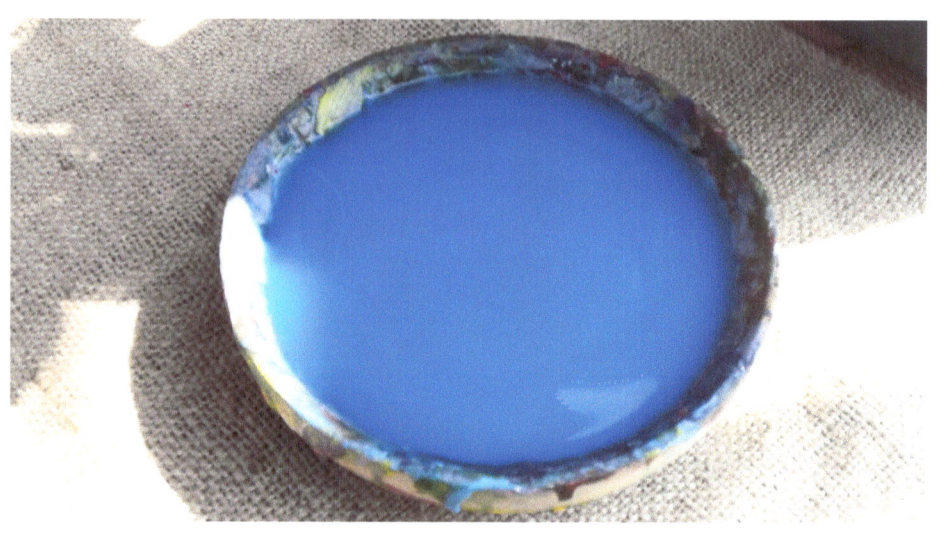

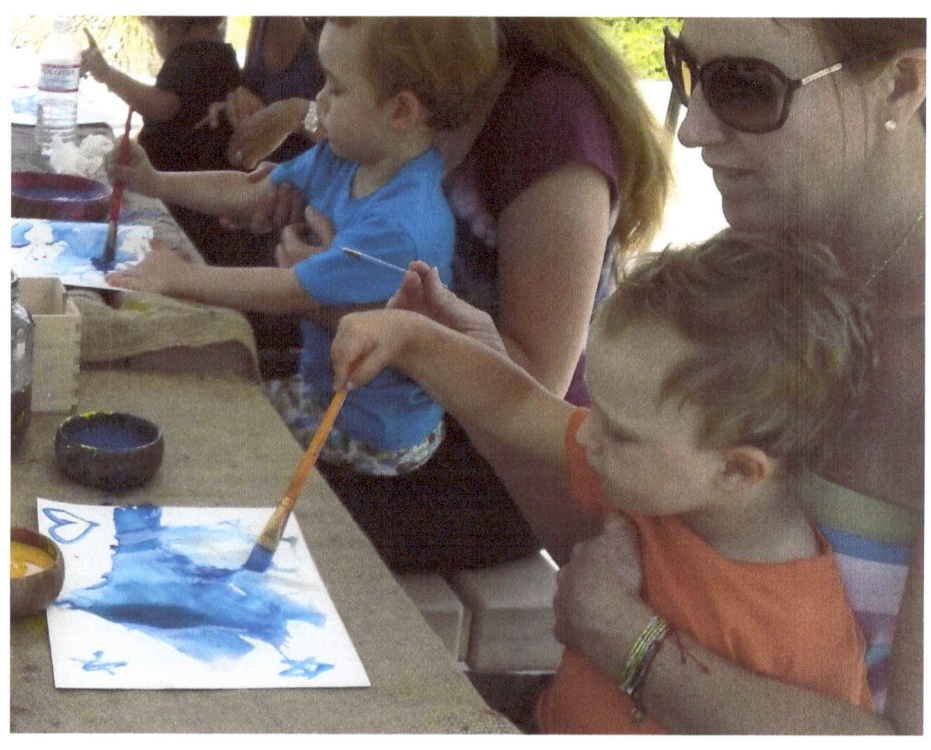

Lesson 4.

Red + Yellow = Orange

Have kids explore painting with these two primaries first, each in a separate lesson of their own.

Secondary Color Mixing

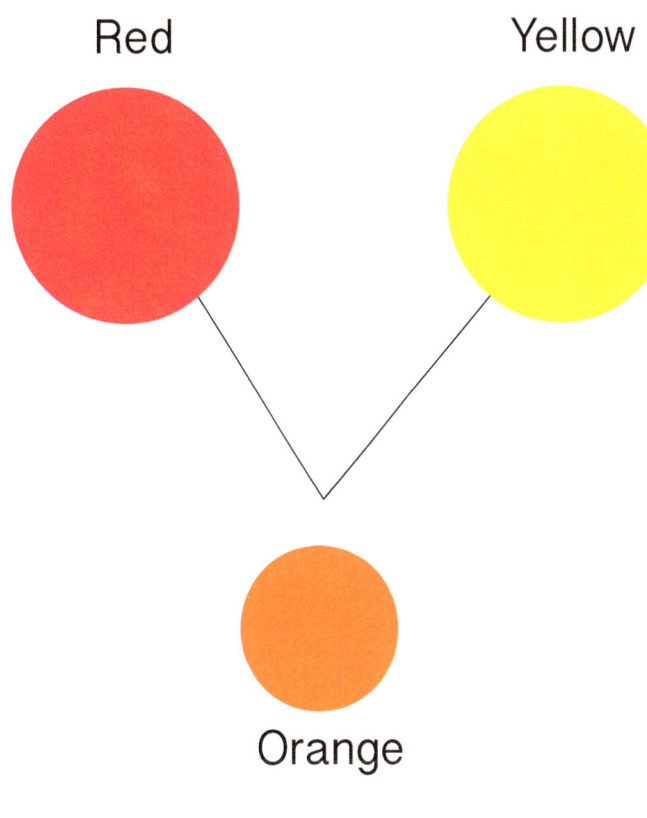

Red   Yellow

Orange

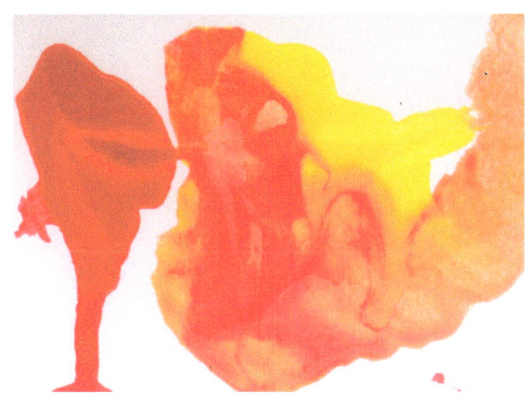

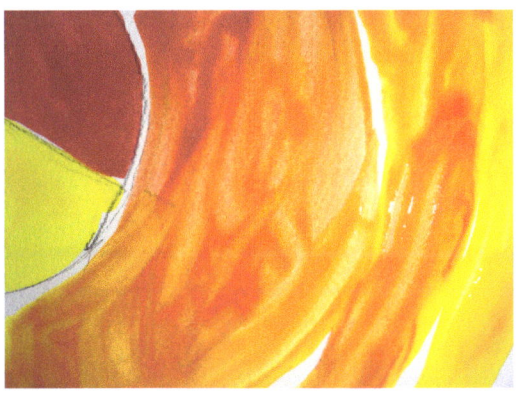

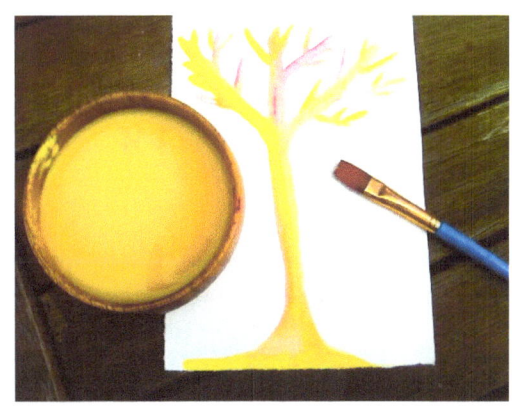

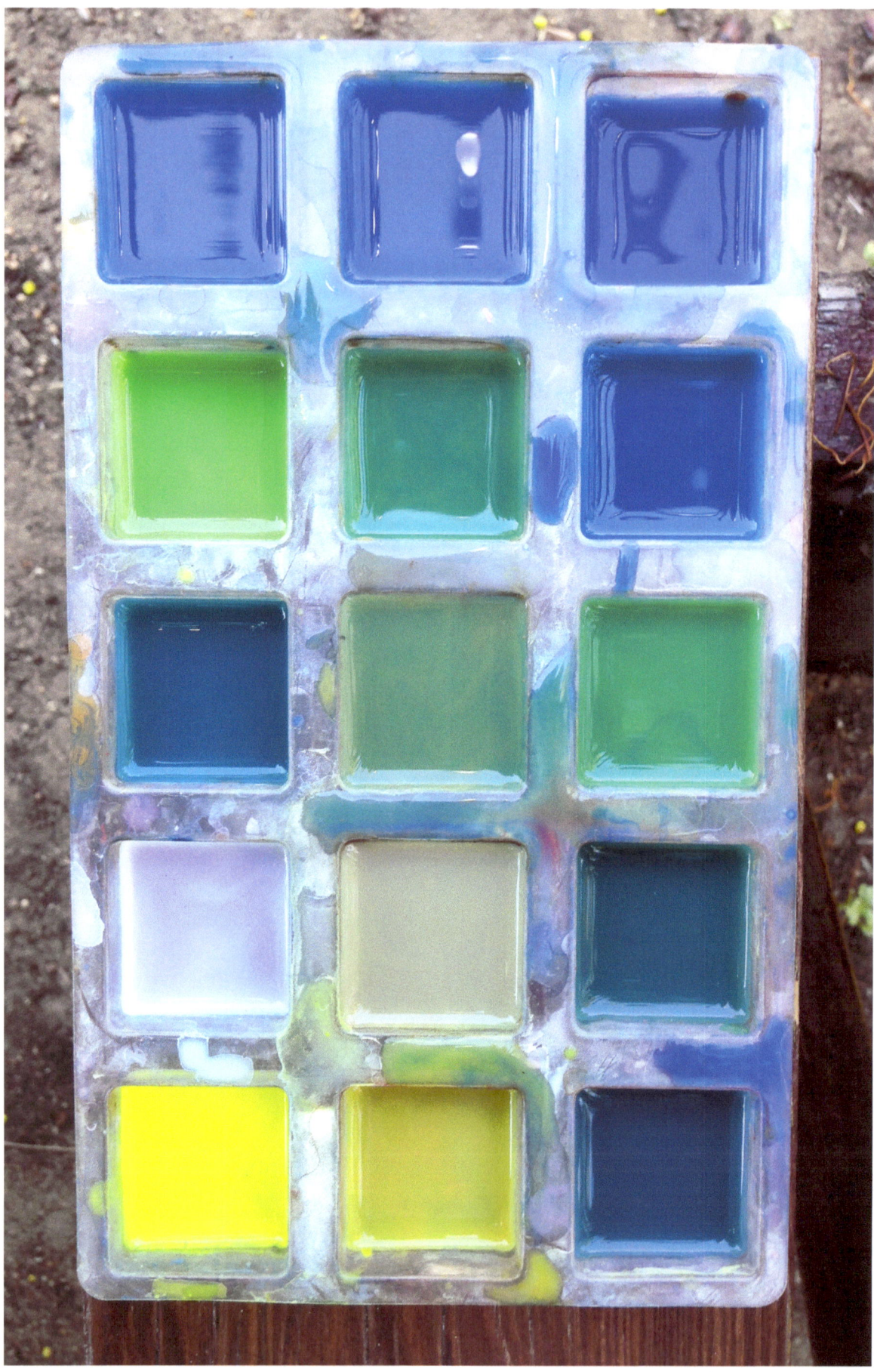

Lesson 5.

Blue + Yellow = Green

Blue 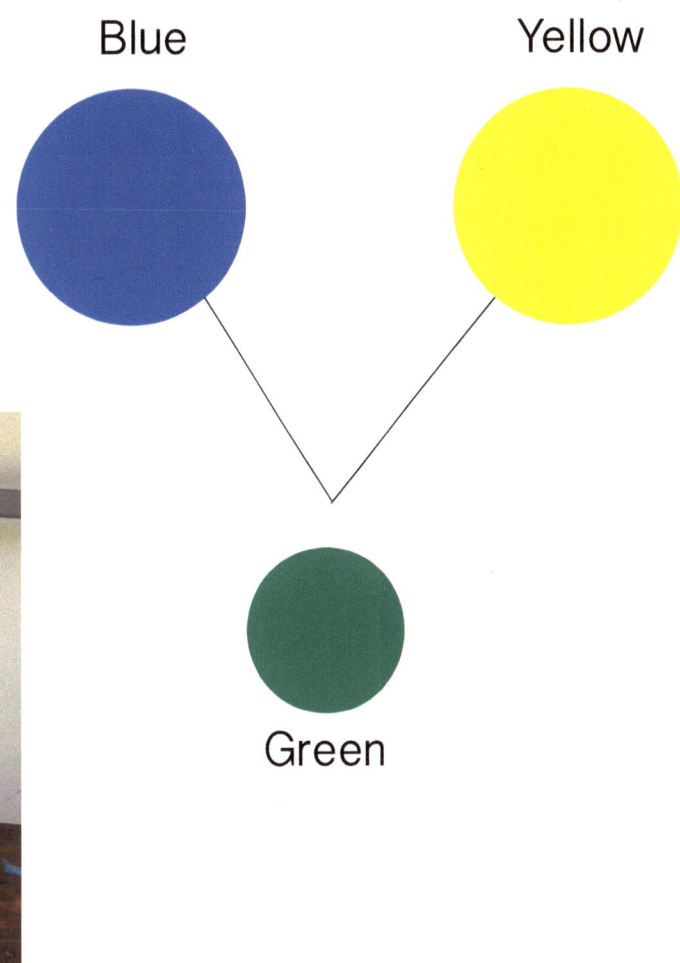 Yellow

Green

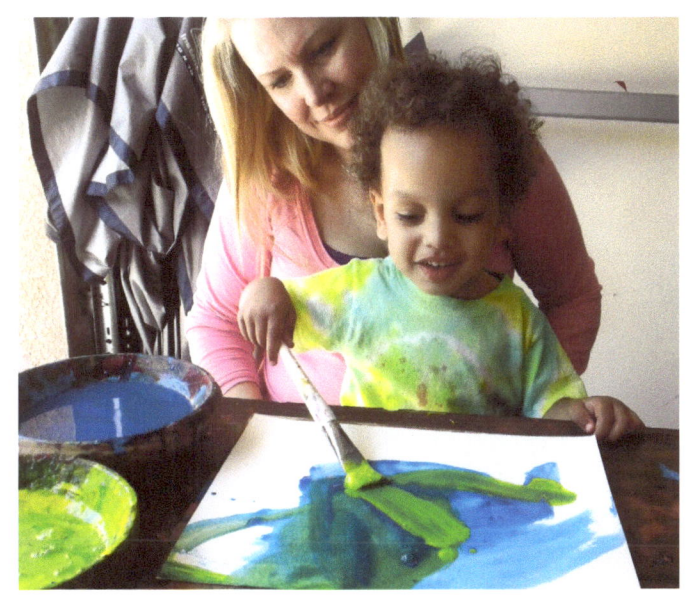

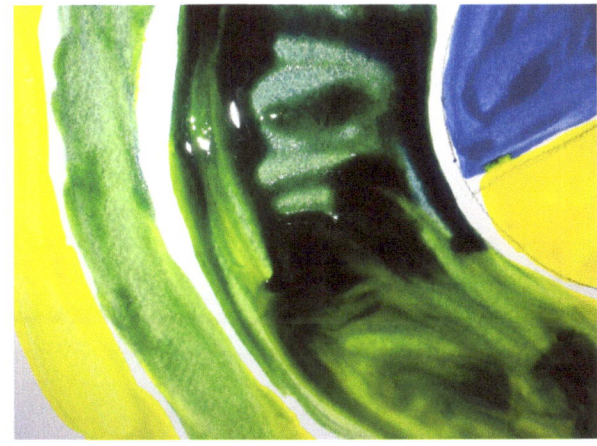
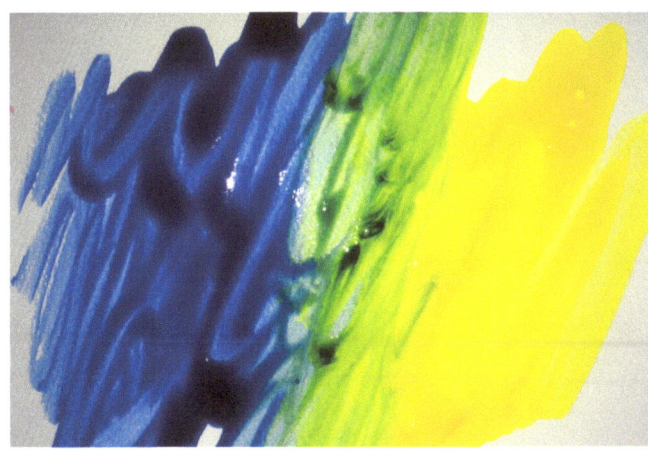

Lesson 6.

Red + Blue = Violet

Red

Blue

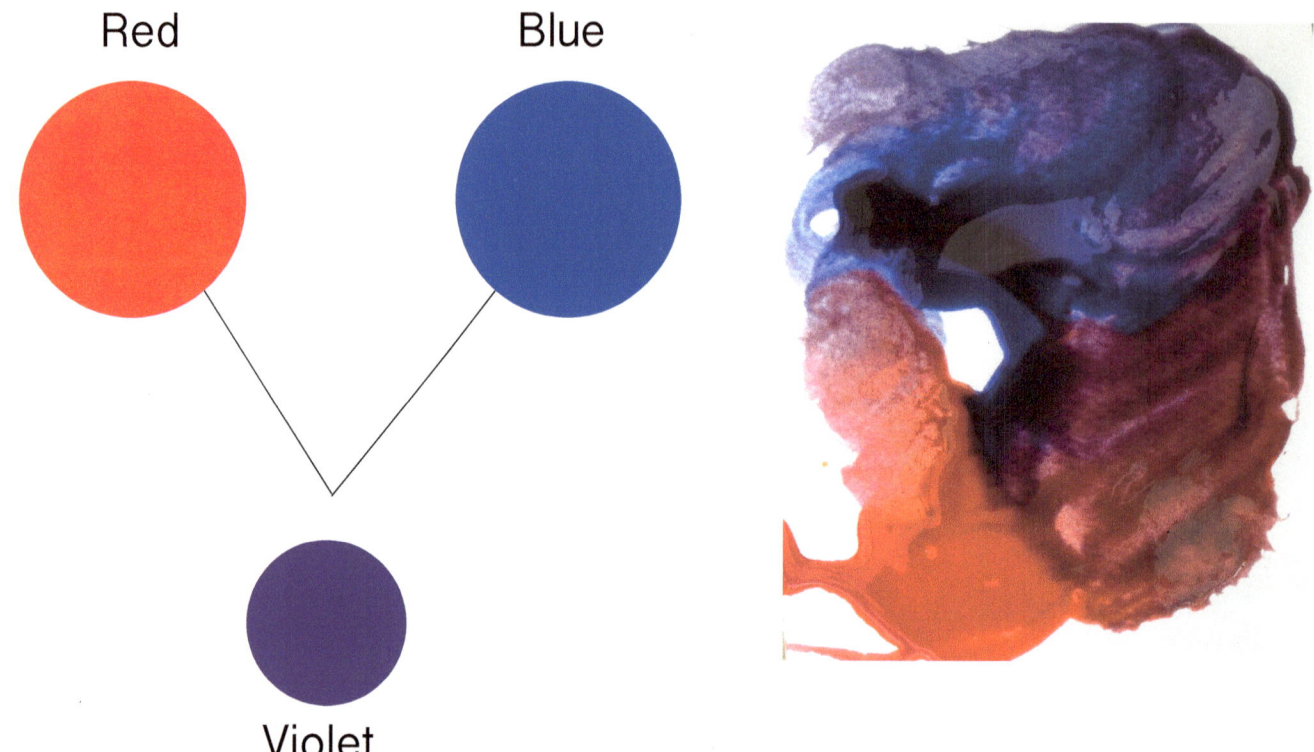

Violet

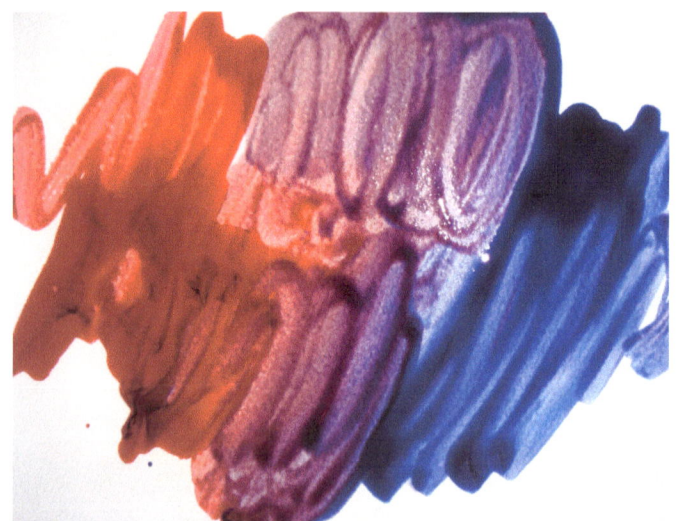

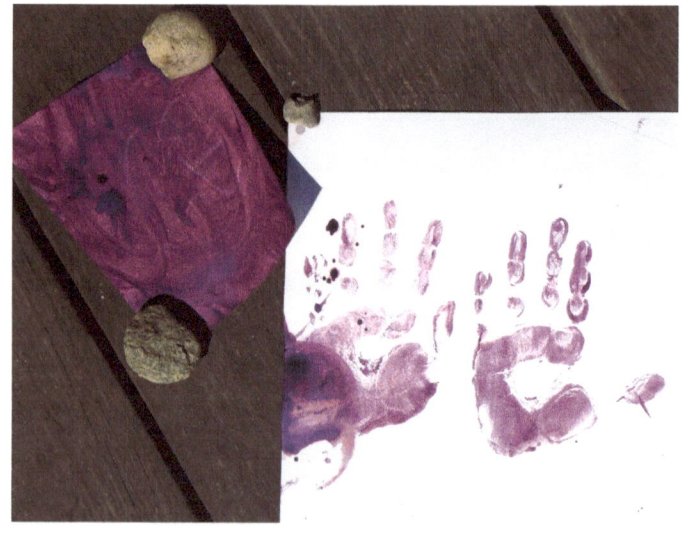

Lesson 7.

Red + Yellow + Blue = Brown

Mix brown with two equal parts of red and yellow, then add a smaller amount of blue. Remember blue is a very dark pigment. Always start with smaller amounts.

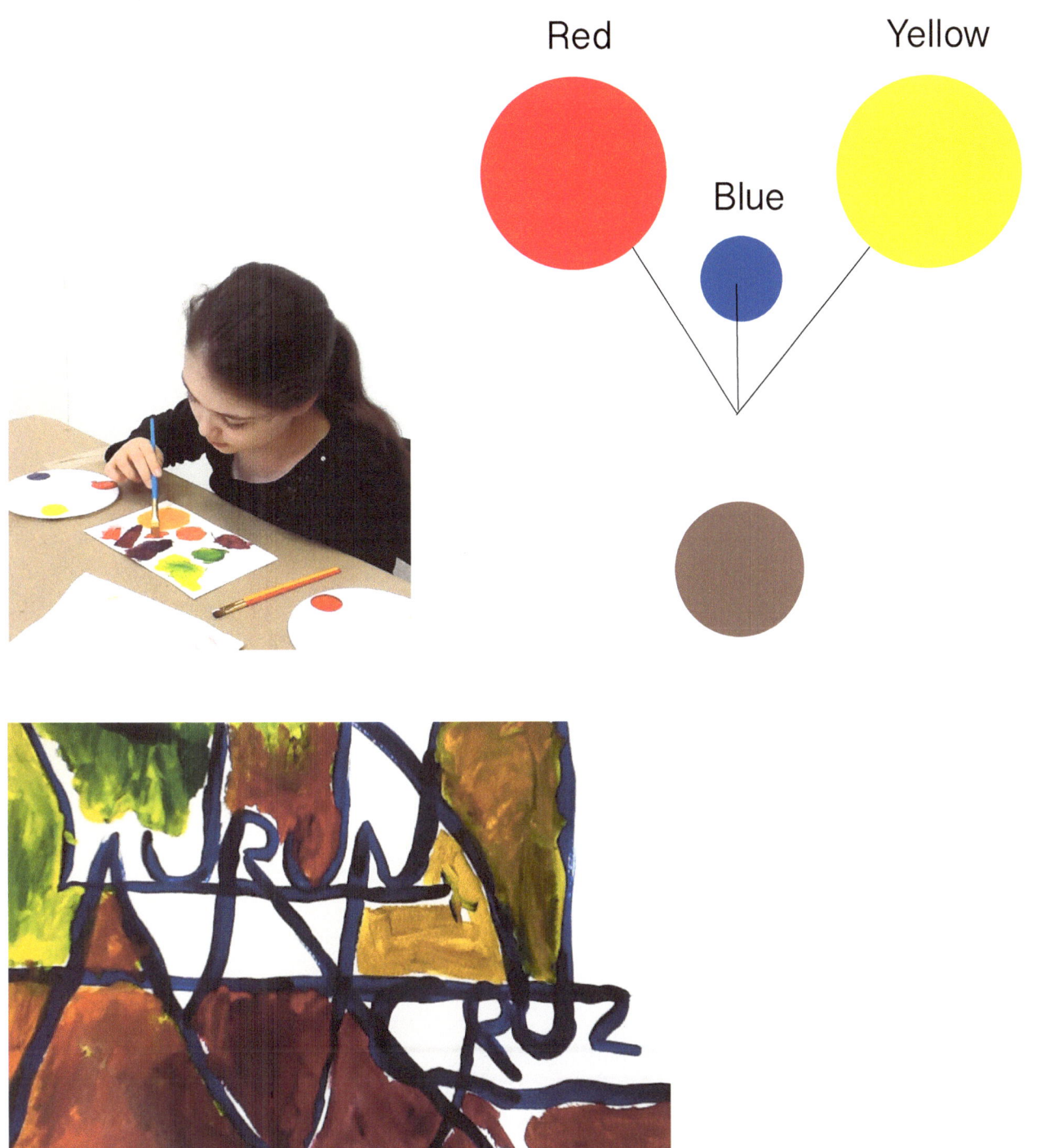

Red

Yellow

Blue

Lesson 8. Value

Have kids explore painting with these two primaries, then challenge them to make three different intensity mixtures, light, medium and dark.

Lesson 8.   **Mix primary colors into a secondary color, then mix three values of dark, medium and light**
Lesson 9.   **Mix primary colors into a secondary color, then mix three values of dark, medium and light**

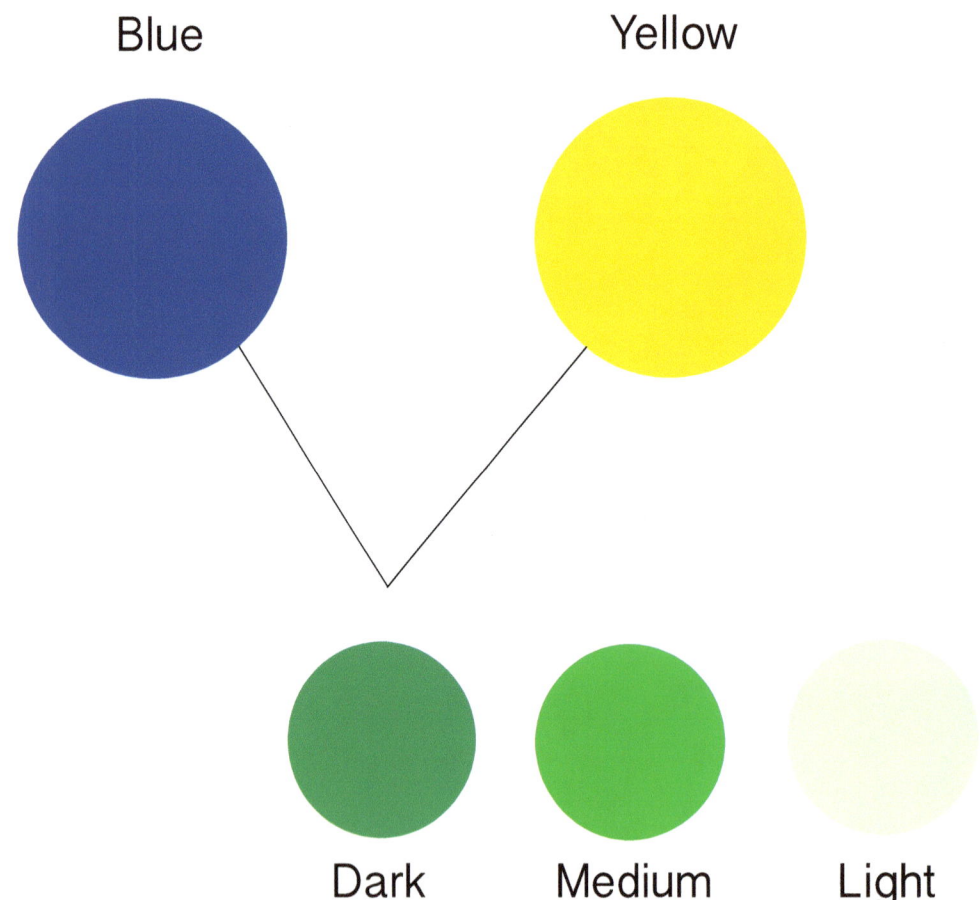

Lesson 9. Value

Value – brightness, lightness, or luminosity: how light or dark a color is.

Red   Yellow

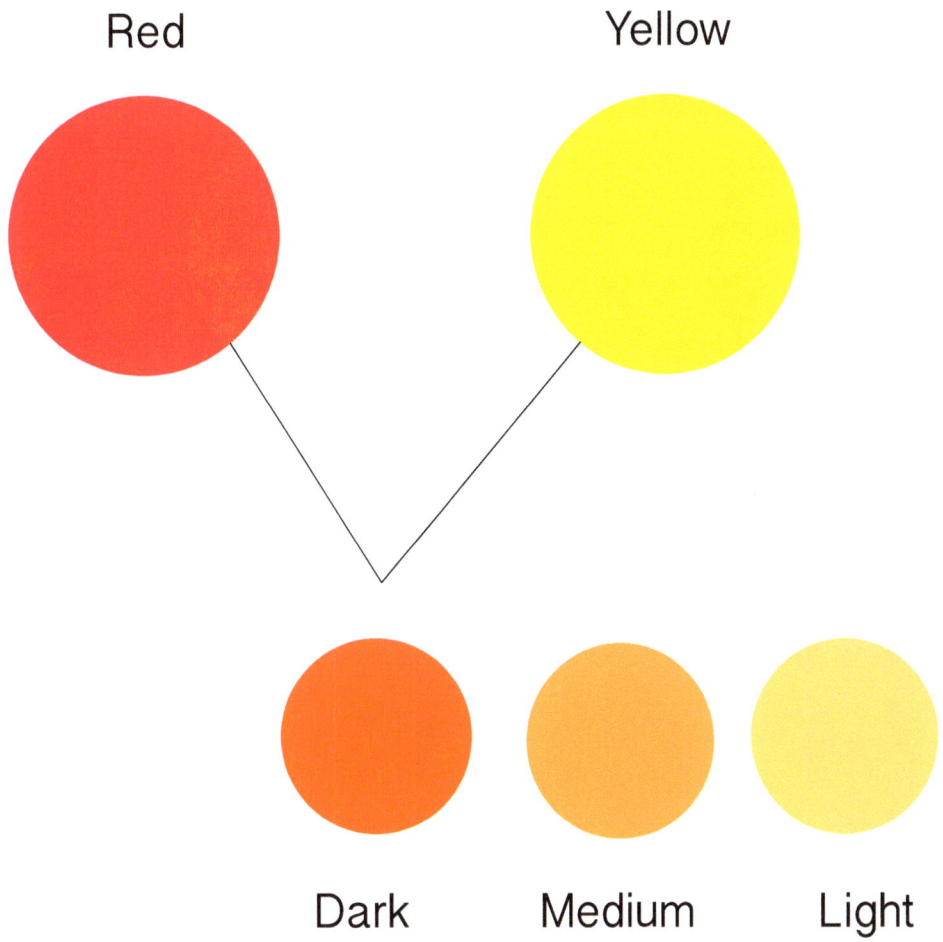

Dark   Medium   Light

Lesson 10. Tint

Primary Red + Blue = Secondary Violet
Secondary Violet + White = Purple Tint

Tint: a color made lighter by adding white.

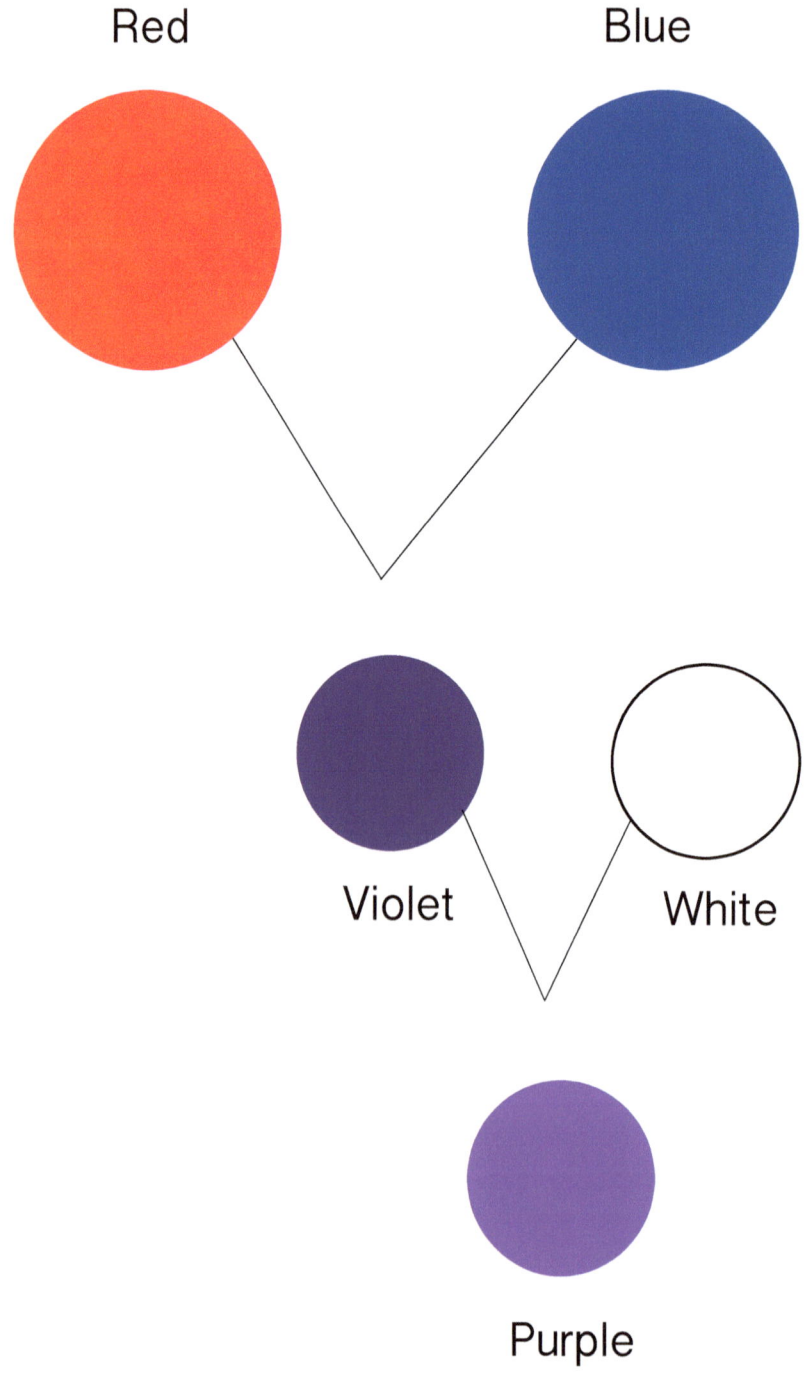

Lesson 11. Shade

Ready-made White + Blue = Gray Shade

Shade: a color made darker by adding black.

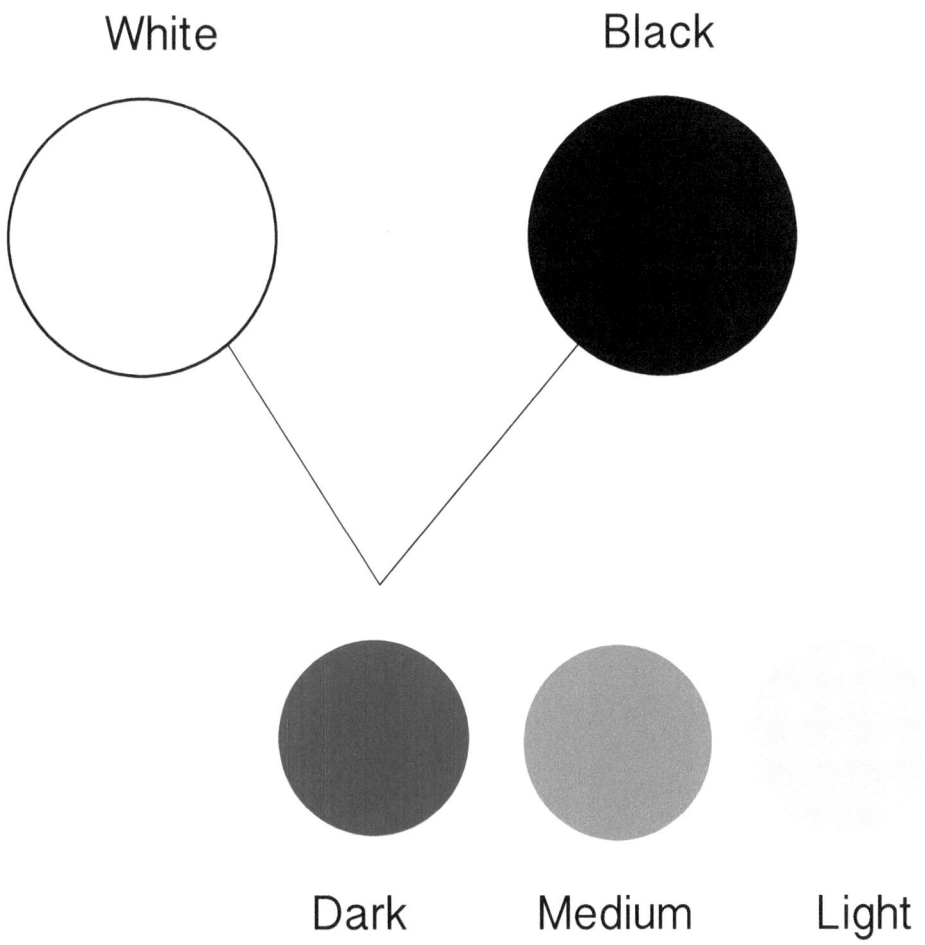

White   Black

Dark   Medium   Light

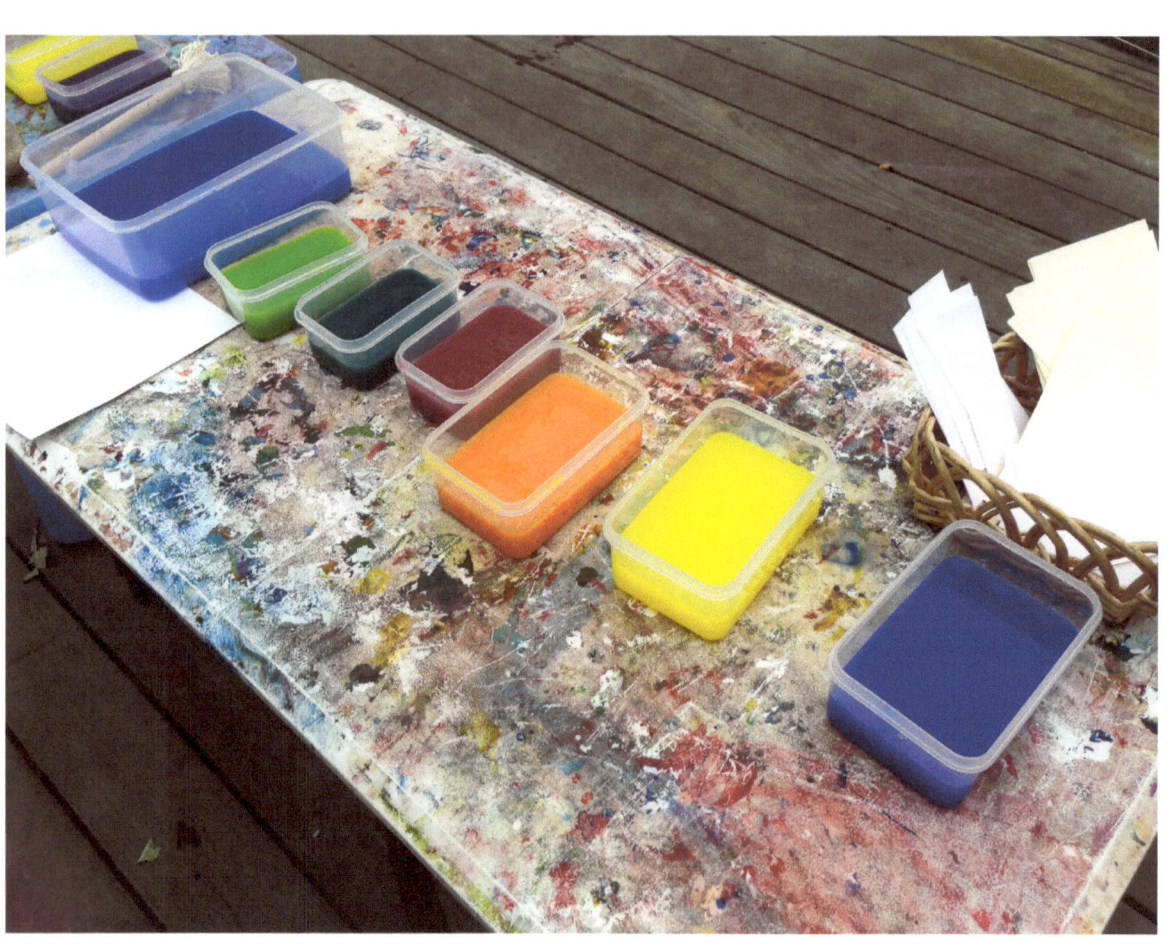

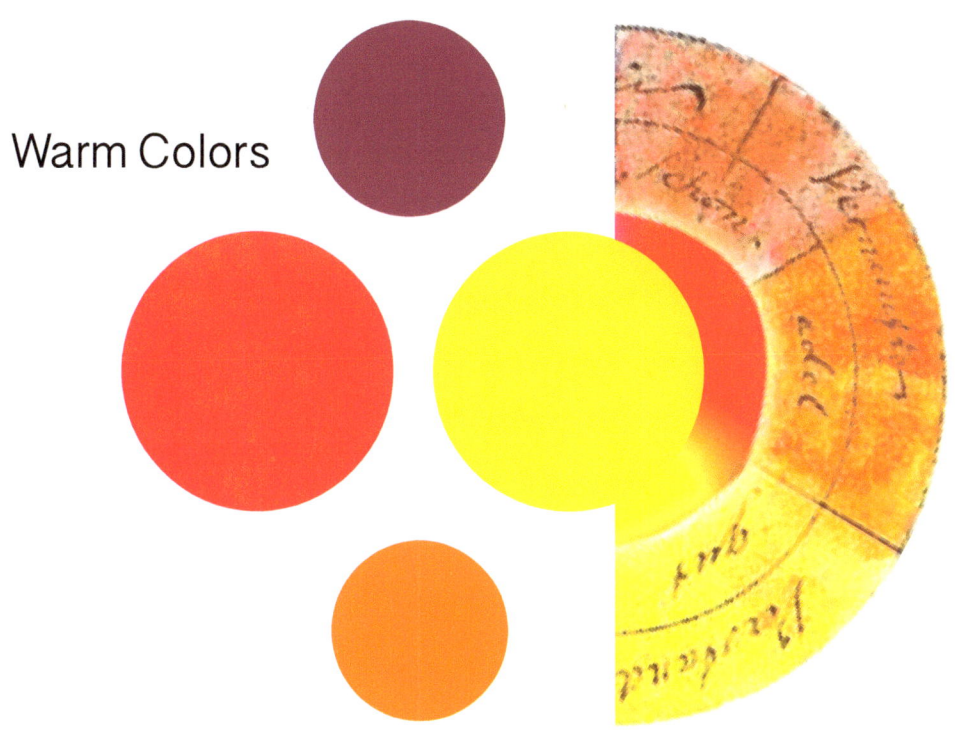

Warm Colors

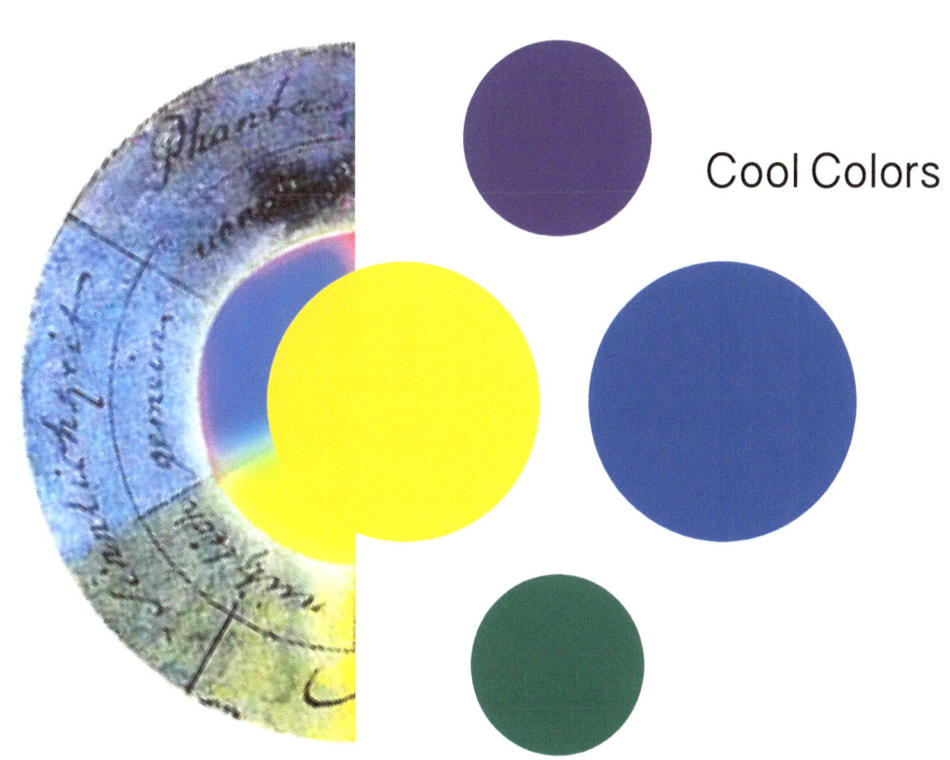

Cool Colors

57.

Author Page

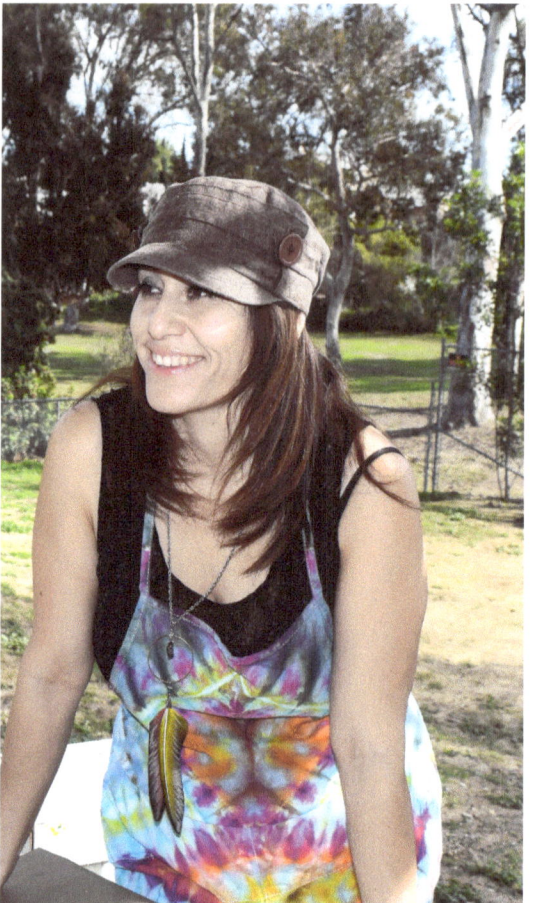

Additional Book Orders/Website Links

Email orders: treepassion@gmail.com
Telephone orders: U.S. (760) 652-5194
Postal Orders: P.O. Box 443, Solana Beach, CA 92075

Order Online: http://www.ecokidsart.com

Linkedin: https://www.linkedin.com/in/ecokidsart

Instagram: EcoKidsArt

YouTube: http://www.youtube.com/user/ecokidsart

Facebook: https://www.facebook.com/nature.of.art

Twitter: https://twitter.com/ecokidsart

Pinterest: http://www.pinterest.com/ecokidsart

Google +: Spramani Elaun

Other Books by Spramani Elaun:
Nurturing Children in The Visual Arts Naturally©
Clay Play©
Kids Painting©
Kids Color Theory©
Kids Doodling to Drawing©

Art Teacher Traning for Montessori Schools and Teachers!

Learn More About Speaking/Seminars/Teacher Training/Conferences/Kids Zone Live Events:
http://www.ecokidsart.com or email: treepassion@gmail.com

Order Acrylic Paints, Watercolor Finger Paints, Painting & Drawing
Supplies: http://www.ecokidsart.com Resources, Website Links

References

Pastoureau M. (2008) Black: The History of a Color

Kenly E., Beach M (2004) Getting It Printed

Solo R. (1994) Cognition and Visual Arts

Solo R. (2003) The Psychology of Art and the Evolution of the Conscious Brain

Gregory R. (1997) Eye and Brain

Karanika M., Article Visual Perception: A Cognitive Process

Hoffman D. (1998) Visual Intelligence, How we create what we see

Brown P. (2007) Toxic Exposures: Contested Illnesses and the Environmental Health

Taylor & Francis (1996) Chemical Exposure and Toxic Responses

Mann L. & Sabatino A. (1985) Foundations of Cognitive Process in Remedial and Special Education

Golding M. & White D. (1997) Color, Web Designer Guide

Finlay V. (2002) Color, A Natural History of the Palette

Berger & Thompson (1995) The Developing Person, Through Childhood and Adolescence.

Lefrancois G. (1986) Of Child, Child Development

Scientific America (1974) Image, Object and Illusion

Sartor M. (1992) Their Eyes Meeting the World, The Drawings and paintings of Children

Wood, Cole & Gealt (1989) Art of the Western World, From Ancient Greece to Post Modernism

Merrifield M. (2005) Light and Shade, A Classic Approach to Three Dimensional Drawing

D'amelio J. (1992) Perspective Drawing Handbook

Cole (1976) Perspective For Artist

Blackstock G. (2006) The Drawings of An Artistic Savant

Eckardt V. (1993) What is Cognitive Science

Barrington B. (2002) Advance Drawing Skills a Course in Artistic Excellence

Hazelwood R. (2004) An Introduction to Drawing

Walker & Roth (2000) Keeping a Nature Journal

Encyclopedia Britannica (2003) Volume 16, Colour

Macropaedia Britannica (2003) Colour and Light

Goldman R. S. (2004) Art Against the Odds

Thomas & Taylor (2003) Drawing Foundation Course

Gombrich E.H. (1950) The Story of Art